2

3

4

Drawings by
Nayla Ruiz-Salfity
(aged 5 years, 11
months).

Photograph by Michelle Steele

Fingertips touch, God sighs,
you give birth.

From 'Birth' by Julia Prescott (page 25)

Musings

on

Mothering

About Pregnancy, Birth, and Breastfeeding:
An Anthology of Art, Poetry, and Prose

Edited by Teika Bellamy

Mother's Milk Books

First published in Great Britain in 2012 by Mother's Milk Books

ISBN 978-0-9573858-0-1

Typeset in Georgia and Unnamed Melody by Teika Bellamy.
Printed and bound in Great Britain by The Russell Press, Nottingham,
on FSC paper and board sourced from sustainable forests.
www.russellpress.com

First published in 2012 by Mother's Milk Books
www.mothersmilkbooks.com

Dedication

This book is dedicated to all those who muse on mothering,
and to my own two muses, Rebecca and Jerome,
who made this all possible.

Sweet, warm, clean, calm, soft,
The scent of their skin on mine
Sends my heart back home.

EMMA COLEMAN

The Hall of My Arms
Painting by Asha Pearse

I am holding out
the glimmering hall of my arms;
showing the lighted room in my head,
which I have carpeted
with your dreams.

from 'Waiting' by Alison Jones (page 18)

Contents

•••

From Broody to Birth

Babymoon

Being a Mother

Of Fathers

Everyday Life

Challenging Times

Remembering Mothers

Our Children

●●●

Nursing on the porch
Painting by Kathy Grossman

Foreword

by Naomi Stadlen

Musings on Mothering is a step forward towards normalizing breastfeeding in Britain as part of a mother's journey through pregnancy, childbirth, and daily life with her child.

In societies where breastfeeding is or was the norm, mothers rarely describe what it was like. Instead, we catch glimpses of how normal breastfeeding could be from casual references. A rabbi living in the first century AD taught that there was a good way for a man to know when to recite his morning prayer: 'For a man who sleeps in a dark house and does not know when the time of prayer arrives: once a woman begins talking with her husband, and the child begins sucking from its mother's breasts, let him arise and recite.'[1] There seems no suggestion that the baby would have woken the man by crying. From this, we learn that a mother breastfeeding her hungry baby while it was still dark must have been such a common event that it was considered a reliable "clock".

In societies — or more commonly in parts of societies — where maternal breastfeeding was not the norm, the usual substitute, before formula milks were invented, was wet-nursing. This has a long history. There is a section in the Code of Hammurabi, which dates from about 1780 BC, covering the rights of parents and wet nurses.[2] Because these rights were considered worth including in the Code, we can reasonably assume that a significant number of Babylonian parents must have used wet nurses.

There is a body of literature which opposed wet-nursing, and which also has a long history. Written almost entirely by men, it promoted maternal breastfeeding. Unfortunately the language was harsh and judgemental. Mothers were reproached if they did not breastfeed their own babies. They were said to be lazy, frivolous, heartless, worse than jackals,[3] inferior to peasant women,[4] and selfishly exposing their babies to the wet nurses' diseases.[5] The fathers' role in hiring wet nurses was rarely mentioned. An exception was Rousseau, who claimed that innocent fathers were tricked into hiring wet nurses by their fashion-loving wives.[6] In reality, the reasons for using wet nurses must have been complex. There would have been social pressures influencing women, as well as their personal difficulties. However, in this literature, genuine problems were simply not addressed.

Perhaps one incidental benefit of wet-nursing was that it kept alive the knowledge of breastfeeding. However, in the twentieth century, formula milks and feeding-bottles became safer and popular, which meant both parents could share formula-feeding. Indeed, both could now earn an income and pay a professional child-carer to bottle-feed their baby. Consequently, girls grew up who had never seen a single baby being breastfed.

Not a moment too soon, La Leche League was founded by seven mothers to provide information on breastfeeding. They quickly realized how important it was to collect fast-disappearing information from mothers about how to breastfeed. Their book, *The Womanly Art of Breastfeeding*, was and still is a revolutionary work.[7] For the first time, breastfeeding was presented as an art, not a set of rules. The first edition was written, not by one individual with her or his personal limitations, but by seven mothers with different experiences. Recent editions have used examples to show how mothers from many cultures have solved a variety of breastfeeding difficulties that can arise. Also, on page after page, we read that mothers find joy in breastfeeding their babies. This gives the book a warm appeal, very different from the pages of a typical breastfeeding manual.

There is another way in which La Leche League is unusual. A new genre of literature has arisen in which mothers describe themselves as subject to their "tyrannical" babies. La Leche League has a completely different approach. The founding mothers recognized how much babies want to breastfeed. They saw that babies' behaviour was rational, and that breastfeeding was much easier if mothers were sensitive to their babies' signals, and followed them.[8]

Although La Leche League is perceived as a breastfeeding organization, the basic position of the League is to see breastfeeding as one part of the whole mothering relationship. The first of the ten concepts underlying La Leche League philosophy is: 'Mothering through breastfeeding is the most natural and effective way of understanding and satisfying the needs of the baby.'⁹ Many mothers who may not have heard of La Leche League have nevertheless reached this same conclusion.

This is the wisdom expressed in *Musings on Mothering*. The anthology provides many insights into how parents feel when breastfeeding has become integrated into family thinking and family life. Here parents express the intensity of their feelings, together with everyday details, a combination that is all too rarely voiced.

I hope these pieces will inspire other parents to muse, and to describe their own experiences. We need more anthologies like this one.

References:
1. Babylonian Talmud: *Tractate Berakoth*, Folio 3a.
2. Code of Hammurabi, 194.
3. *Lamentations of Jeremiah*, 4.3.
4. For example, Tacitus, *De Origine et situ Germanorum*, chapter xx.
5. For example, Nicholas Rowe, English translation of Quillet's *Callipaedia*, Book IV, page 16.
6. Jean-Jacques Rousseau, *Emile*, chapter 1.
7. La Leche League, *The Womanly Art of Breastfeeding*, first bound edition 1963, and eighth edition 2010.
8. For example, *The Womanly Art of Breastfeeding*, eighth edition, 2010, chapter 4.
9. See www.llli.org/lad/talll/philosophy.html.

Teika, Jerome, laundry basket
Painting by Angie Stevens

Introduction

by Teika Bellamy

Socks, socks everywhere
But not a matching pair.

Silly rhymes, poems, and stories have always been part of my life. When I was young, my family and teachers encouraged my writing and I enjoyed this "messing around with words" very much. As I grew older and became intensely absorbed in the busy world of work, there seemed to be little room for this type of creativity. However, I can still remember the books I read while on the tube, or in the snatched minutes at lunchtimes. Escaping into these fictional worlds provided me with reassurance and inspiration: such is the power of story.

When I gave birth to my first child and began in my new role as a mother, the silly rhymes, poems and stories returned to my lips and my daughter seemed to enjoy the happy prattle that emanated from her mother.

We both rejoiced in our bond, yet she seemed to be growing and thriving at a greater rate than I was! It was only when I attended La Leche League meetings, and found myself surrounded by women who accepted and supported my mothering choices, that I began to relax into my new role. I quickly became a member and looked forward to the monthly meetings that strengthened and sustained me through the many, many sleepless nights that I was experiencing.

Before I had children I had assumed that motherhood would be rather dull — that it was simply a never-ending round of chores with little time or space to think or do. Yet here were mothers — most of them at home with their children — doing a huge amount of creative work, be it with their hands or their minds.

I wanted to give something back to the charity that had helped me so much, so I thought of ways to fundraise. A few months after my son's birth I conceived the idea of this anthology and as I went about my everyday motherly work (baby in sling and laundry basket under my arm) I gave serious consideration to my plans. While my little one slept I worked on the project, and slowly and gradually, it began to happen. He is now a walking, talking toddler who likes to help me with the laundry!

Although I had always been sure that I would receive enough submissions to fill a book — since I knew of many artistic and literary mamas involved with La Leche League — I never anticipated the huge response I actually did get. Checking my email inbox was a daily delight as I received wonderful submission after wonderful submission.

I relished the task of fitting the submissions together, and quite early on I decided it would be natural to start the anthology with the haiku 'Conception' by Michelle Sorrell, and fitting to close with 'The Ballad of the Beach' by Marija Smits.

In between these two bookends there is a huge range of poetry, prose, and art in various styles. Each chapter has its own theme and there is a rough chronology to the book. The first chapter, 'From Broody to Birth' deals with the months leading up to the birth of a child. 'Babymoon' follows on by describing some of the intensity and passion of the time immediately after a baby is born.

The next two chapters, 'Being a Mother' and 'Of Fathers' explores some of the facets of parenthood, and 'Everyday Life' details some of the wonderfully intimate, funny and frustrating moments that make up day-to-day life.

In 'Challenging Times' mothers speak of illness, loss and sadness. Their words make for powerful reading. Whatever the challenge though, we are reminded that 'Mothers are wonderful warriors' by Anna Morton in her poem 'Warriors of Love'.

In 'Remembering Mothers' there is loss too. Yet there is much joy as well in this chapter. In her poem 'Things My Mum Used to Say', Emma Coleman reminds us of the humour inherent in any human relationship, not least in the mother-child relationship.

The book ends with musings on 'Our Children' and a montage of images that highlights the stunning work of some "crafty mamas".

Undoubtedly though, the most memorable aspects of editing the anthology were those light bulb moments when I just knew I had the perfect image to accompany a poem, and *vice versa*. Katrina Soper's senryu seems to have been made for Allen Ng's photograph of a father and child, and Kathy Grossman's painting *Young mother in the fabric souq* is a glorious partner to Jessica Starr's poem 'Motherhood'. Likewise, Kirsten Foubister's poem 'Thursday morning 11 a.m.' goes hand in hand with Angie Stevens's *Sleeping* doodle, and Maryam Mirza's drawing of her baby feeding is a beautiful accompaniment to Alice Allan's poem 'Passion'.

These, and many of the other pairings, serve to illustrate the fact that so many of these life experiences are shared between mothers — and yet each individual's "voice" is unique. Running through the whole book, like a golden thread, is La Leche League. Time and again mothers write with great warmth of the support they received from this charitable organization.

Editing this anthology has been a wonderful experience. I've been in contact with many amazing people, and made some great new friends along the way. Indeed, some of the poems, phrases, and images within these pages have lodged themselves so deeply in my consciousness that I now consider them my own companions for life. If just one phrase, poem, or image connects with you in some way, I'll consider myself richly rewarded.

Enjoy!

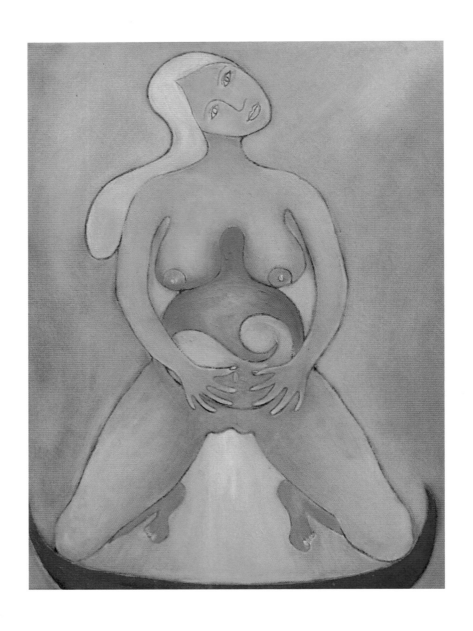

Earth Mother Goddess
Painting by Alex Florschutz

from Broody to Birth

•••

Conception

Plant in me a seed
I shall make it wonderful
The best yet to come.

MICHELLE SORRELL

9

Broody

Waiting,
Hoping,
Anticipating,
Praying for your existence.
Amongst a crowd,
But still alone.

Still waiting,
Upset and disappointed,
Annoyed too.
I'm confused.
I feel as if you're there. Can you hear me?

Wealth,
Fame,
I've been chasing them for so long.
Achieved a fair share too.
But now I feel as if it is all immaterial.
It doesn't matter anymore.
I just want you,
My true happiness.

It isn't pride,
I don't want you because others have their own.
It isn't arrogance,
You will inherit that from your father not me.
Just make sure you inherit his smile too.
What's the matter?
Are you scared?
Or is it me?
Do you not want to be with me?

I can't wait to hold you,
Love you.
You are all I need.

Waiting,
Hoping,
Anticipating.

Waiting for you,
My baby,
My own.

JUMARA NAZMIN AKTHAR

New Year in a Strange Place

In a fold-up bed in a spare room,
stars tangled in nets our only light
bruised and sputtering like carnival lanterns
out along a pier some long-gone season —
cold, unbreathed-in, nobody lives here
but you and me, for one night only

and when we rise, snow-crystals forest the glass,
the room, blankets folded, a smudge on the mirror,
hardly notices us. I don't know it yet
but this is the place he began,
squib of fire, our son, this first bright day of the year.
We are a mystery of three as I close the door.

PIPPA LITTLE

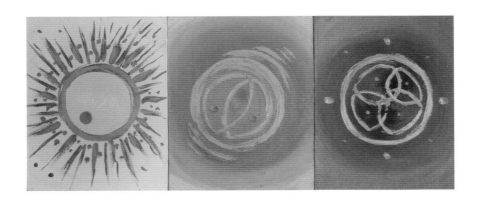

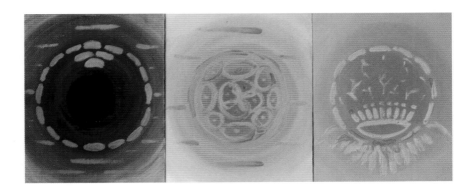

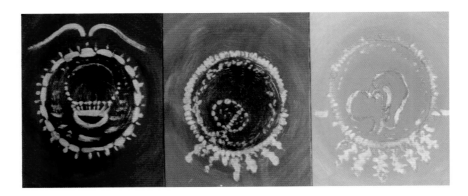

In the Beginning 1 (top)
In the Beginning 2 (middle)
In the Beginning 3 (bottom)
Paintings by Alex Florschutz

Child in Utero

Slip a lens
through the uterine wall
and there discover
a foetus,
exposed
with miniature arms
like sticks,
veins and vessels
criss-crossing the body
like roads on a map;
a luminous life force
priming a frame
with blood lines tattooing fingers
and nipples raised as orbs
as the embryo floats,
arm raised above closed eyelids
caught in an optic glow.

JOHN ROE

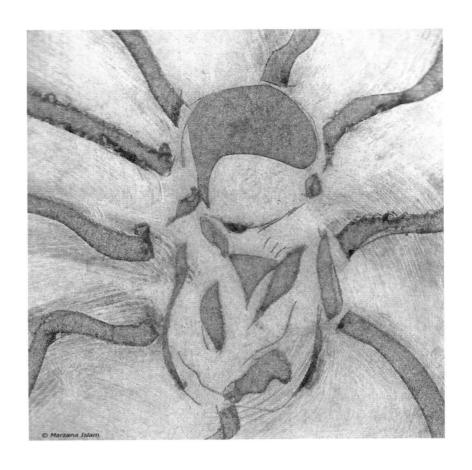

Collograph by Marzana Islam

Ultrasound

We were spies on her world —
her safe house of skin. She
was etched in silver: moving, human.

She swam in a booming cave,
fathoms down. Heavy rope mooring her.
Round face, round eyes, ooh of mouth.

Gingerbread baby, currant eyes.
At home, I twist wool around needles,
craft garments, every stitch a wish.

ANGELA TOPPING

Dreaming

You are a chrysalis,
dreaming of wings,
if we could achieve
synthesis,
of ancient and new
the reality would be this;
wide awake, clear eyed,
clutching at the certainty
that once you flew,
waiting
for metamorphosis,
hoarding fragments
of all you knew.
This is not sleep,
but the land of dreams,
where everything is real,
yet not what it seems.

ALISON JONES

Waiting

I am waiting for you to begin,
when you are ready, I know
you will make the journey;
set forth against the tide and ride
into the space that I
have been preparing for you.

I am holding out
the glimmering hall of my arms;
showing the lighted room in my head,
which I have carpeted
with your dreams.

I am stretching
the tall feather of a seed,
freeing particles to ride the wind,
breathing warm currents to speed
the bearded travellers home.

I am waiting for you to begin;
here in the gleaming gathering space,
mapping geography behind
my eyes;
waiting to see your face.

ALISON JONES

Photograph by Alejandra Cerdeño Lance

How the Spell was Broken

Epiphany

When I discovered I was pregnant I felt amazed, unsure if this was real. Holding my tiny bump of ten weeks, I experienced a kind of epiphany, realizing there was a life growing inside me, one which was my responsibility. The enormity of this knowledge brought tears to my eyes. Elated, great swathes of love translated through my body to my unborn child. Like a mantra I whispered;

'I will take unending care of you, do not fear.'

Our tiny son somersaulted in his watery world as we watched in awe at this miraculous image on the screen. Our foetus refused to stay still. A month later, on learning we were to have a boy, faint flutterings surprised me as our son flexed, strengthening his muscles. These soon became strong kicks as he danced in his secure, peaceful domain. In yoga nidra I imagined his fingers and toes growing, his eyes and hands opening, his organs developing, his translucent skin forming; I meditated for his safe passage, praying for his health.

Preparations

Feeling strong and alive, I prepared for a natural birth, practising yoga, going for long walks, swimming and reading about birth. Seeking a last respite as a couple my husband and I retreated to Westray, a beautiful, remote Island in Orkney. Practising yoga from the shelter of our little cottage, I watched as the waves crashed violently against the rocky cliffs, contemplating their movements as I internalized the wisdom of my late Nanna's words;

'Contractions are like waves, still at first, developing in strength, before the crescendo, then calm again...'

Like the waves, labour pains existed for a purpose, an intricate part of nature's plan. I would live through them free from medical interventions.

Hearing newborn lambs bleating through the stormy nights I fought my maternal urge to rescue them, as I felt the increasingly strong kicks of our son inhabiting his ever-shrinking, ephemeral world. My nesting instinct kicked in as we returned to our everyday lives. I ritually cleansed our new surroundings — a larger family home. Waddling on local walks, images of my little boy running through the woods, around the lake, delighting in nature, flickered through my mind. Yet he wasn't quite ready to enter this new, physical world; my due date came and went. We waited. He would join us when he was ready.

Eventually mild contractions began swirling through my body. Gentle swimming eased the pain. Back home Buddhist chanting music calmed me as I instinctively rocked from side to side, leaning on the birthing ball. Later, I laboured actively in hospital, composed and confident. With a sudden, violent gush my waters broke, traces of meconium disturbing my equilibrium. Informed meconium in the waters could be a sign of foetal distress, so my midwife strapped me to a foetal heart rate monitor, my movements now restricted to the bed. Trapped, I moved inwards to the rhythm of the waves crashing inside me, removed from the electrical, bright, clinical world.

On another level of consciousness I retreated into my own safe cave, my husband guarding the door. His massages on my lower back reminded me I was not alone. My eyes firmly closed, I swayed; from deep within me sounds came unbounded, accompanying my contractions, increasingly strong and dominating. I knew my husband and the midwife were close by, so I could call them, *if I needed to*. I trusted and read my own body. This special zone was rudely interrupted as I heard my new midwife suddenly exclaim;

'You're being very musical!'

Almost violently this human voice pulled me back into that other world I had laboured hard to mentally retreat from. I could have hit her. Although unintentional she had broken the spell, the peaceful zone shattered.

Back to the machines, bright lights and human conversation. And with it the pain.

CAROLINE COLE

To read more of Caroline's birthing story please visit her website: www.stoneageparenting.com

The Crowning

Primeval energy fixes her to earth
like an oak tree rooted deep.
Rush upon rush pours through her body.
'I am not pushing, I am being pushed.'
The pod swells, skin prickles, vagina burns.
'It is not possible!'

Gently now comes the head.

'I can't... I can't...
I can!'
The flame-red peony opens
its thick wide petals spread
a child's head like a hard bud in the center.
It is circled by a burning crown
studded with fire
glorious at delivery.

SHEILA KITZINGER

Birth
Batik by Sheila Kitzinger

Birthing Voice

The wailing of the women of earth haunt my mind,
The universal cry of age old knowing mingles with my own.
I am connected to you all, before, now and future.
This moment, when the instinct cannot be pushed aside;
It is the strongest, the rising light of pure existence
Of life — beginnings and renewal, a complete letting go.
Our raw state of femininity unties itself from all its bindings
And burns through the room,
And out into the universe.
The earth, a mother too, cries out with us
Relieved to again hear our voices mingled with hers, as one.
A second of being able to hold us within her beauty once more,
Feeling our connection,
The mutual love, rise up again completely irrepressible.
The voice is released, the one we have never heard
And cannot control
Yet understand and know better
Than anything that has come before.

ANNA MORTON

Birth

In the cliff, a cave:
paths wind back in to darkness
behind the retina of the split rock.
A small flame, a pool of water
and the breath-held moment
of imminent birth spreads
outwards from the shadows,
spills into the sunlit space.
The bright beyond holds
tenderly this point
where past and future cross.

There is comfort in chanting,
a single note flung
towards the vault's echo.

A daughter all your life
you are now crossing over to the other side
of motherhood. Only now we begin
to understand things we did not know
we did not know —
where love comes from
the struggle of creation
the passage from one dimension
to another.
Fingertips touch, God sighs,
you give birth.

JULIA PRESCOTT

Sweet Breastfeeding Latina Momma
Art quilt by Karen Bachman-Kells

Babymoon

●●●

Baby

Baby warms me now
Heart to heart with heat of love
Chilly winds don't touch.

BENAIFER BHANDARI

Baby's First Feed

Baby born one moonlit night
Was greeted by a lovely sight;
Open arms, a smiling face
That shone with tender, loving grace.

Weary, hungry, needing rest,
He turned towards his mother's breast.
There he drank her sweet, warm milk,
As rich as honey, smooth as silk.

Sated, sleepy, so well fed,
He dozed upon his comfy bed.
There he drifted off to sleep,
Amidst the shadows, soft and deep.

MARIJA SMITS

Hello Mother

The moment I held you in my arms,
Small body pulsing with new life,
I knew;
Knew you did not belong to me.
We were still one, as we had been all those months,
But those eyes, looked wisely up at me
Our first sight,
And confirmed all my suspicions;
That you were you
And I
Was your vessel
Your privileged guide, not your owner.
If anything, you, from that moment owned me
Or rather, set me free.
I simply became myself.
No lightning, fireworks, brain-exploding eureka moment,
Just completely normal.
This scene was already reserved in time.
The earth turned and welcomed us both anew
Hello Daughter, Hello Mother.

ANNA MORTON

Passion

Pulling you to me I make ready, shed my clothes
Rush to silence your sharp cries of desperation.
You are intent, pursued by wolves,
And follow, blind, the smell of your salvation.

Comfort is close but I'm untested;
You don't know to trust me yet.
Urgently you root and grasp,
Gape and plunge, and suck and suck...

Call and response, you ask, I give.
A throbbing surge wells from the deep;
You rear away and gasp for breath;
Milk sprays like gentle braille upon your cheek.

Your body softens as you suckle now, and fists unclench.
Slowly your fullness makes things safe again;
A small hand is smoothing the roundness of my breast.
Drunk on love you fall away and rest.

ALICE ALLAN

Long feeding
Drawing by Maryam Mirza

Babe in arms

Enveloped in my arms
I gaze in awe;
Mesmerized by your beauty,
Delirious with love as I drink in your delicious smell
And meet those magnetic eyes that hold mine, that know my soul.
When your sweet little mouth latches to my breast
We are both nourished in body and mind,
Connected and complete.
Selfishly I delight in your need for me,
Greedily I relish the intimacy; the warmth of your skin, the gentle
Kneading fingers and those soft, satisfied sighs.
How clever Mother Nature is
To awaken such protective love
To keep us close
Quietly getting to know each other
Easing us into a world apart.
When I first took you to my breast
I felt truly alive
For the first time in my life I knew myself, my purpose,
Such eternal peace!
Living is life and you are life!

RIONA MACKIN

The Beauty of Breastfeeding
Photograph by Theodora A. A. Ireson

The Other Side of Sleeplessness

I can still remember the initial shock of it. Being woken repeatedly, night after night, never quite getting into a deep sleep cycle, never quite grasping that complete relaxation that goes with perfect rest. Without regularity or apparent sense, my baby frequently and piercingly woke me from sleep. She woke to be nursed, to be held, to be rocked, to be changed. She woke for comfort and for company. She woke because she needed me, and my role as her mother did not stop when the sun dipped below the horizon. A 24-hour job, I was on call all the time. But the sleep, oh the sleep. I needed it, it needed me, and yet we were kept apart by the ceaseless needs of my newborn baby.

I stumbled through my days, feeling as though I was walking through treacle. I felt defeated, frustrated. Usually an organized, clear-minded, thinking woman, I became foggy-headed, repetitive in my speech and limited in vocabulary. I struggled with simple tasks and limited car journeys to just a few miles for fear that I might put myself and my baby in danger. We took to walking in all weathers. My dreams of taking up new hobbies during my maternity leave seemed laughable as I found that all I could do was care for my baby, and where possible, look after myself. Each day I wondered whether tonight would be the night: would she let me sleep a little more tonight?

Sleep is a favourite topic of conversation among new mothers. How much a baby is sleeping, or not, can even become a way for mothers to compete with one another — the length a baby sleeps somehow becoming a sign of a mother's competence. Or conversely, the one who has had the least sleep somehow receives a badge of honour. Especially in the early months, sleep can be an all-consuming subject. At the behest of babycare books or other advisers, mothers may spend countless hours and endless amounts of energy trying to mould and manage their babies' sleep patterns, trying to achieve the coveted holy grail of "sleeping through the night".

Few people stop to consider that not only is there a biological reason babies wake frequently in the night, but actually this sleeplessness has another side. Being woken at night is exhausting. Sleeplessness can feel like torture, can make a mother sensitive to the point of bursting into tears over a mere trifle; it can make every molehill seem like Everest. But there is more to being woken in the night than being tired. Although it seems absurd to say it, to some extent those moments can be re-framed as an opportunity rather than a trial.

I have asked mothers, 'What's nice about being woken in the night?'. After an initial shocked silence, mothers talk about the timelessness, the stillness, the peace of being alone with their babies in the wee small hours. While the rest of the house and the world snoozes, mother and baby are together, alone, curled into one another like jigsaw pieces. Some mothers talk of loving the chance to listen to nighttime radio, of having time to meditate or be alone with their thoughts. Others roam the house, check emails or write letters. I sometimes say, 'I'm too tired to be inspired!' but I know several mothers who find the nighttime to be a particularly creative space. Other mothers relish the singularity of being alone with their babies. One mother explained, 'When he's awake at night, it's just me and him, you know? There's no one else there.' No one else to tell a mother what to do, no disapproving looks or comments, nothing else to divert the mother's attention — at night she is there for her baby and nothing else. All she needs to be is a mother rather than the thousand other things she is expected to be during the day.

Those are the quiet moments. A baby's night waking isn't always peaceful: sometimes the baby is screaming and a mother is at her wits' end to comfort her baby. What could be special about those gruelling nights of struggling to latch the baby on or pacing the floor with an unhappy, crying child? I believe that these times are essential — a golden opportunity, even — to building an authentic relationship with our children. As many people will have experienced, when our friends tell us only the good things about their lives we feel somewhat shut out: the relationship doesn't feel real. It's only when a person really opens up to us and reveals their own pain and struggles that we begin to connect through empathetic understanding. The relationship develops a new texture that was not previously there. In much the same way, our unending presence for our babies in the night allows us to reach out to them with compassion. No one likes to be alone when they're unhappy. Human presence helps, and we can give this to our babies even if we cannot solve the problem that is at the heart of the crying. Through sharing his unhappiness we develop an unbreakable bond. Later we can reflect on the times we shared, and a mother who has comforted her baby during his misery knows that she has done all she can for him and given him the gifts of company and empathy. Developing my relationship with my baby in this way is worth more to me than a few hours' sleep.

Sleeplessness isn't easy, but it also has its unexpected reverse side. People often refer to the first weeks after a baby is born as a "babymoon". It's a special time, where the minutes seem to have elongated and nothing else matters except the family. When my third baby was born, I stayed on or near my bed for the first week. I called it my "John and Yoko" period — it was my opportunity to totally hunker down and focus just on my baby. I happily received guests and presents from the comfort of my bed and relished the care my husband and other children gave me as I bonded with and cared for my newborn. In a similar way, a bad night (or several) can have the effect of focussing a mother's priorities. When I'm tired I have to decide whether I really need to keep that appointment on the other side of town or can it wait for another day? I can happily accept the invitation to lunch at a friend's or an offer of dinner dropped off at home, guilt-free, because I know I need it! If we have the flexibility to clear the diary, have a "duvet day" and spend the day quietly in the house, a bad night can be a great excuse to dispense with the rest of life's responsibilities and concentrate completely on the baby and self-care.

In the midst of tiredness it's easy to forget that this is a short phase in a child's life and in our lives as mothers. Even if, like me, your babies don't sleep through the night until around the age of four, it still is only a fraction of their lives. Three children later, being woken at night now feels routine to me; a full night's sleep is a shock. But I say to myself that it's all part of the experience of being a mother, and one day I will look back and miss those soft warm bodies cuddled against my own and wonder where the time has gone.

LISA HASSAN SCOTT

A Moment in Time
Drawing by Teodora Graham

Photograph by Jo Welch

Being a Mother

●●●

I Am All

I am food
I am drink
I am comfort
I am security
I am warmth
I am love
I am your mother

NIK HARRIS

A Womanly Joy

Breastfeeding was an uphill struggle following the birth of my first child. With determination and caring support, once we'd overcome our initial hurdles, it became second nature. At my breast I met my baby's need for food, for comfort, and for security. I gave him my milk and I received, in return, the pleasure to be had in knitting bonds of love. In those quiet moments I became his mother.

As soon as we'd got the hang of how it worked, snuggly breastfeeding was the easiest and most effective way of satisfying my son's needs. After a separation and a tricky start altogether, I felt I had to hold my little boy and be with him most of the time. This was for my own peace of mind, as well as to keep him happy and establish an adequate milk supply, which I did by letting him suckle very often and whenever he chose, both day and night. His need to be with me was as intense as his requirement for the calories he was getting from my milk (and the quality of that milk was better than any second-rate copy). But, I was surprised by the intensity of my own response, on both an emotional and physical level.

When I'd considered having a baby, I'd composed a long list of fears that outweighed any sound reasons for wanting one. I was afraid that my desire for a child might be little more than a whim and was fearful of the reality of strife and hard work. The joy that came with motherhood, particularly in the communication of breastfeeding, was a pleasant surprise and all the hard bits were worthwhile.

The process of breastfeeding is relaxing and happily that's nature's design. For a start you're sitting or lying down. With an increase in maternal levels of natural opiates during lactation, the release of oxytocin (the hormone of calmness and love), followed by a release of prolactin, there comes a letting go, then a serenity that helps enormously to make mothering deeply satisfying. I understand that there are morphine-like substances in your milk that during breastfeeding calm the baby too. In this quite blissful state of relaxation, I would stroke and hush my beautiful son for a large part of each day. I loved cradling his tiny warm body, unworried by the mountain of undone chores, letting the course of life find its own rhythm. That gentle pace was something I was unaccustomed to after working in a busy office in central London. Breastfeeding slows you right down to invest the gift of time in your baby.

I've breastfed three children now and my first baby will be fourteen this year. While there's a lot more to being a good parent than breastfeeding, I'm pleased to say that trusting my instincts with regard to keeping my babies close, feeding on cue and bedsharing wasn't a sign of weakness on my part. I like the analogy from *The Womanly Art of Breastfeeding* (that I heard at my first La Leche League meeting) of fruit ripening on the tree, its source of nourishment, but spoiling if left on the shelf. "Giving in" to my babies was a fine start to mothering.

BARBARA HIGHAM

Brilliant Embrace

One sip to the head
Another to the heart.
Suppression and release —
This animalistic act
Returns me to something
I can't remember or don't,
But aims me straight ahead.
A tender grasp,
A hard, pounding fist,
At times, asking for more.
What else can I do,
But bring you close and
Offer myself profoundly
As much as I opened up
To bring you into being.
It is all so easy and so hard —
Holistically, happily, heartbreaking.
A swift season of utter abandon
To you. You who will grow,
Fresh and strong from me, and leave.
Someday we will marvel together
Eyes filled with wonder,
As your new one or young child,
Touches your hair,
Digs in deep for more,
Searching for sustenance,
And everything we can't explain,
Which all starts here.
We will see each other
With changed eyes
From the irreplaceable gift,
Which keeps on giving
Through generations of mothers
Choosing to lay it all down.
Give, give, giving, never gone.

ALYSHA JONES

Clockwise from top left: Photograph courtesy Caroline Emptage, photograph by Theodora A. A. Ireson, photograph by Philip Ivison, photograph by Jo Welch, photograph by Allen Ng: www.ang-photography.com, photograph courtesy Ruth Asch, photograph courtesy Lucy Holmes, photograph by Fujiaki Uesugi. Centre: photograph by Jose Alberto Garibaldi.

Motherhood

Six months ago
I first put on
my mother hood.

It felt strange at first,
weighing heavy
on my head
and on my shoulders.
I worried how it looked
to others.
Did I wear it right?

Gradually,
I felt more
and cared less.
I caught my reflection
in my daughter's eye.
It looked good.

Six months ago
I first put on
my mother hood.
It suits me.

I forget what I looked like
without it.

JESSICA STARR

Young mother in the fabric souq
Painting by Kathy Grossman

From Me to You

More than just food
Vital nourishment
Warmth
Security
Comfort
To calm all fears
To ease all pain
An unbreakable bond
Unconditional love

You returned it all
Tenfold
You taught me how to be a mother
They were special days
Thank you

CLAIRE MILLS

At Last

She feeds her baby
and it is the first loving touch
she has ever felt
in her bruised and battered life.
She strengthens and nourishes
her little one,
and introduces him to love and trust
and he does the same for her.
He thrives, and so does she,
for the first time;
for the first time, and forever.

CATHY BRYANT

Mothering From the Inside, Out

When I looked into the eyes of my first baby I realized I hadn't reckoned on her at all. This little human who had come to live with me had her own wild spirit and had no intention of following my path and plans. Nature gave me a stubborn one to start with, just to ram the point home, but each child has taught me that while nurture is a huge part of becoming who you are, some things are innate. Living as part of a mother-child dyad, so closely locked together with another, I've grown to both appreciate the disposition and quirks of my children and to smile ruefully at my own peculiarities. Somewhere between the painful breasts of the first few weeks and the unravelling of weaning, my babies taught me that being fully human, with all those imperfections and eccentricities, was to hold the key to a unique response to the world and that nothing could support creativity more successfully.

This might seem like a lot to gain from simply feeding a baby, but the milk is only a tiny part of it. In the early days, breastfeeding was the entire relationship I had with my babies. And as they grew and became more social and had other means of communication, the breast was our shorthand, our intuition. With each baby came not just a different style of feeding, but a unique way of being in the world which demanded my acceptance. Their little characters were writ large in their feeding behaviour and I've been amazed at the differences between them and how those early displays of preference and emotion have developed throughout childhood. Even writing with the broadest of strokes, their differences are apparent.

Breastfeeding has taught me to relax and allow my children to be. They demonstrate a need of some kind and I try to help them, a philosophy that has continued beyond the limits of the breastfeeding journey. Being openly encouraging of my children's quirks seems to me the greatest way to instil self-confidence and self-belief. It's one of the many reasons I home educate, to give that uniqueness time to flourish and take root before the world piles in. Mothering from the inside out means honouring the nature of my children and having confidence that in celebrating their differences, their world will be of their own making and therefore, a happy one.

But unfortunately not all of us have been mothered in a way which respects those deepest parts of our personalities. The world as it was presented to me required competitiveness, toughness and ambition. For me, school was the beginning of a race for the top; homework came first, certain subjects were worthwhile, but others were irrelevant. For a long time my apparent confidence could be blown away by the slightest breeze because somewhere along the way my self-worth became tied up with achievement. I became further and further removed from who I really was. Being mothered from the outside in, created a belief in me that living successfully in the world required certain attributes and since I lacked those naturally, I'd better develop them — or fake them. Not great for a daydreamy child who preferred her imagination to real people and who had a natural disinclination to competition.

But my own children caught up with the truth. I learned that if I can embrace the various passions, obsessions and habits of my daughters, shouldn't I extend the same love and consideration to myself? There's great joy as you finally breathe out and say, 'You know what? That's not who I am. I don't care about that. I care about this.' Moving your energy and attention from over there to over here gives boundless freedom. The slowing down of life which happens with the birth of a child, the hours of stillness required to breastfeed, led to a turning over of my heart, a re-examination of all I had been told.

My husband, thank goodness, hadn't married me for my towering ambition! Knowing my heart's real desire, he built me a writing hut. That little yellow pile of wood tucked into the corner of the garden, has womb-like qualities. Sometimes I can almost reach the daydreamy child within. I'm getting there.

LYNN BLAIR

Earth Mother

Here in the sitting room of your East London home
your brand new daughter sleeps on my lap
her downy skin silken beneath my fingers
her half-moon nails just tiny dots
on her peacock-splayed toes.
Stretching her arms above her head
she draws her knees towards her tummy
yawning contentedly.
Outside a noise startles her;
she cries, but just for a second.
Frowning crossly she returns to her sleep.
You sit at my feet oiling her creases
and take her to your breast with an age-old confidence
that has eluded generations.
I am amazed at your newly-found skills —
though not surprised.
You are of the Earth.

JOSIE DEVINE

What My Daughter Told Me

Slow down, you told me.
Before you, I moved and swirled through my life, trying to capture the
oyster they all promised, never starting and never stopping. Sure that
if you came along, I would have to give up the world that I was trying
to save.
But you came and the world was mine. Saved and perfect all in one
day.

Let's dance, you said.
The steps so small and perfect that only you and I could ever know
them.
Each day, a new step of the dance to learn. My mind was blown.

Speak to me, you whispered.
I didn't know I had the power to speak without parting my lips. That I
could know a person so deeply that her soul would actually be my
heart.
You came from so far and near. Further than the smallest star, but
closer than my own skin.

Listen, you said. You know all there is to know already.
The world just sped by while you and I sat in our own little pocket of
life.
I was mindful without even practising.

You made me still, strong and beautiful.
I am braver than I even knew.

I am not perfect, I said.
You are enough, you replied.

SHIREEN BABUL

The Mother-Soul

The moment a child is born, the mother is also born. She never existed before. The woman existed, but the mother, never. A mother is something absolutely new. ~ Bhagwan Shree Rajneesh

What does it mean to be a mother?
I often struggle for the words to address this question, to adequately describe the profound transformation that occurred to me more than seven years ago.

It is as though when each cell of my children's bodies was formed within my womb, a corresponding cell of my own body was also transformed. In building a baby, I also built a mother. In mothering my children, I also nourish my own mother-soul. Becoming a mother is a two-way mirror of co-creation.

Mothering for me has been a profound experience. A soul-shaping, deeply fulfilling, essential process. It is what I am about. I was not expecting this. Let me be clear, mothering is not my everything. And it certainly doesn't come easy – rather it challenges me daily to my core. It has chased me to utter despair and back again. With each child I have had, I mourned the prolonged putting aside of certain parts of myself. I cherish little pockets of respite from the endless mental and physical intrusion on my previous, independent sense of self, which the daily reality of mothering requires. I do not find that the daily drudge of mothering comes easy: I do not feel like a natural. But the soul side – that is different.

My mother-self is like my twin soul which I never knew I had until it was activated by the tiny germ of a child growing within my womb. I was birthed as a mother on the day I birthed my first baby. My experience of mothering is what Jung would have called an archetypal experience. Being a mother is part of my being. I am a mother in every cell of my body, at work, across the oceans, in my deepest sleep.

Once we have experienced this transformation on a personal level, we suddenly recognize it in others — our friends, our sisters, our own mothers, as well as every wolf, cow and cat that we see. We understand what drives her, her basic motivation, her deepest feelings for her children.

And know that I do not speak lightly of this. I know what it is like for the mother-soul not to be awakened. I know that whilst it is generally a natural occurrence, it does not always happen. A shock to the mother, the separation of mother and child, a traumatic birth, depression — all can delay or sever this bond.

I have experienced the awakening of the mother-soul twice. But I have three children. For my middle child I did not experience it. For three years I simply acted as if I had experienced it. I consciously went through the motions of mothering, of being the matrix, but with my head rather than my heart. The soul sense of mothering was not there. It was horrible to feel detached, especially knowing how it felt to be attached to my firstborn. But it emerged. Suddenly, one day I was aware that it was there. It is a little more tentative than my other two, but it is there, the mother-soul.

***

Matrix is the Latin for womb, and the root of our English words matter, material and mother. It is also our term for energy field or underlying fabric of being. This feels instinctively right as a description of what being a mother is, for me: I am a matrix, a sustaining and nurturing energy force. A feeling which the acts of natural birth, breastfeeding and co-sleeping have all acted to reinforce.

Joseph Chiltern Pearce, author of *The Magical Child* explains that the mother offers three things to the developing child: 'a source of possibility; a source of energy to explore that possibility and a safe place within which that exploration can take place.' This confirms to me that mothering is really energy work — requiring soul energy and physical energy — which is why it is both as challenging and rewarding as it is.

One of the most insightful discussions of the spiritual energy of mothering that I have discovered is in the writing of Rudolf Steiner. He developed the idea of a Madonna's cloak, which surrounds the child for their first three years, experiencing itself as still part of the mother. It is 'the outstreaming of the mother's soul [which] can be pictured as forming a protective cloak around the baby, radiating love and protection. For the young child [the] Madonna's cloak is a spiritual reality. It enfolds him in warmth and deeply affects him.'[1]

As mothers our fundamental role is that of being physical and spiritual energy in which our child may grow and develop their own vital energies. This takes courage, wisdom, consciousness and a conviction about something which our culture has little understanding of.

Another vital part of our journey as mothers is to learn to wean with love. To build our children's own physical and spiritual strength, so that they are flourishing. And then, to learn to pull our own nurturing energy back, little by little, in an age-appropriate way, until they are able, in good times, to sustain themselves, safe in the knowledge that they might return to the matrix at any time. This is the goal of mothering.

In order to do this, our sacred lesson is to learn to nurture and sustain ourselves. We cannot nourish another if we deplete ourselves. If the river runs dry, the crops will fail. Always, always, a mother must return to self-care, to nurturance of herself: she must prioritize tending the wellspring of her own health, her body, her soul. So when we breastfeed we must ensure we are well-nourished, well-hydrated and well-rested. We must nourish our spirits in whatever manner speaks to us. Health for mother, and child, rest on the balancing of energies, of giving and receiving.

Mothering is sacred work, spiritual work, hard work. As mothers we get to be co-creators in the magic of the universe. Let us honour this task, ourselves and our children. Let us provide a culture and environment for the mother-soul to flourish: for ourselves, for all mothers, for our children, for the future of our species.

LUCY PEARCE

References:
1. Joan Salter, *The Incarnating Child*.

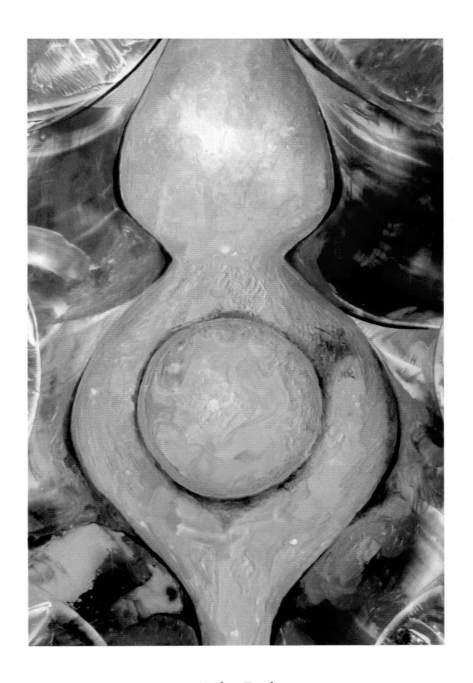

Mother Earth
Encaustic art by Judith Kuegler

Photograph by Allen Ng: www.ang-photography.com

Of Fathers

•••

My baby, snuggling
Learned to trust that her daddy
Would never fail her.

KATRINA SOPER

Green Peppers

It was the last time I saw you
Before you knew you were a daddy.
I had gone to the doctor
To confirm what I already knew
And I said I'd honk if it were true.

So there I came honking and honking.

Into the driveway
And you were watering
The green peppers.

And you said,
'Well, what did the doctor say?'
As you stood there staring at me
Before you knew for sure.

And I just started to cry
Standing there with my baby magazines
And development charts and diaper coupons
From the doctor's office.

And there you were going to be daddy
With the hose still running
Holding me who was going to be mommy
At last.

KATHY GROSSMAN

Letting Out the Long-Held Breath

A Father's Reflections

We are currently expecting our third child in December, and two nights ago I felt the baby kick for the first time. What's really great about having a second, or third child, is that the worry about how to help with labour is tempered with the knowledge of what will happen at the end of labour. After two hours or ten hours, however long it takes, a baby will be born. My baby. A sibling for our two boys, another grandchild for our parents. And I cannot wait.

Oh so vividly do I remember the awe, the joy, the fear and the sudden intense connection with my parents and all the generations before me, and the generations to come, when I first held my newborn. To hold a newborn baby for the first time, still slippery from birth, is surely one of life's most amazing miracles. My life is changed in an instant, and will remain in this state of change, possibly forever. The earth no longer revolves around the sun, but rather around this child, MY child. Cradling my boy I let out the breath that I didn't even know I was holding — and had been holding for the past nine months. Looking down at his head, and across at his mother's eyes, we meet in perfect accord. Surely we are the luckiest parents in the world — for what have we done to have been so blessed with this child?

To witness birth and to hold such newness in your arms is to know a strength of love previously unimaginable. To my wonderful wife, for the births we've had, and to those still to come, I thank you. I truly love you.

ARTHUR MOLLOY

A Sentimental Sestina

He raises his head from the test, eyes bright.
You're going to be a mother.
I'm going to be a father.
He is radiant.
Our baby, our baby.
He is overwhelmed with love.

Now I share the centre of his love.
But there is room for all. I am bright
With the joy of our baby.
I am becoming a mother.
My womb growing, myself growing radiant
He is becoming a father.

I wish to be a good father
He says. I'll show love
To the woman who is radiant
Whose eyes are bright,
Who will be the mother
Of my unborn baby.

His baby, my baby, our baby.
He is a father,
Just as I am a mother
To the evidence of love.
Cannoning across the screen, joyful, bright
The image is radiant.

We are radiant.
A family now; a couple with a baby
Three pairs of eyes, one new, are bright
Unshed tears of father
Brimming with love
Unshed tears of mother.

I wish to be a good mother
For my daughter to be radiant
In our newfound love
She is wise, this newborn baby
She already knows her father
At the sight of him, her eyes are bright.

She too is bright
With unquestioning love for mother and father.
We are radiant with unconditional love for her, our baby.

LAETIA HAWKSBY

One Soft Light and All the Right Cushions...

I wake up in the quiet bedroom. Hal is about to wake up, I feel it. Quiet, quiet, quiet — and then I hear it, a little cry. Out of the Moses basket, hold him close and go down to the sitting room. God bless Jason — he has everything ready for me! One soft light in the corner, water on the coffee table, all the right cushions in just the right places. It means so much to me. You find out a lot about yourself when you have a baby and you find out a lot about your partner too. Jason became a father at the self-same moment I became a mother and immediately, things between us changed for the better. We have a baby's needs to put first, but those aren't just crying and nappies. How could I have got the knack of breastfeeding without Jason calmly listening to the midwife while I was consumed by hormones and emotion? Then, the moment I latch Hal on, all the moisture leaves my head and it's Jason who brings me water. Jason helps me so I can help Hal, and so we three became a family.

Now Hal and I take our place in the middle of the sofa, so far the only place we can breastfeed — variation and dexterity are still to come! I wedge Hal in place with the cushions — that firm little orange one in the shape of an owl is perfect for bridging the V-shaped pillow — undo some buttons and begin. After a few false starts, we get it right, the milk comes down, the glug-glug-glug subsides and all I can feel is tiny Hal, snuggled in close to me... and my shoulders. I consciously drop them — ah! — and lean my head back.

Now is a special time; a time to be quiet with my precious baby, a time to think — so much to think on now my life has changed forever! I have been looking forward to this all day, through the interruptions, through the interest and interference, through traffic and telly and Jason not being able to find things in the kitchen. He's made every meal since Hal was born and I'm so grateful for that. It's not just the food. Cooking is just one way of showing me I'm not alone in this — of sharing this almost overwhelming experience with another adult. Likewise, Jason doesn't get up in the night with us anymore but here he is, still supporting me — look, one soft light in the corner, water on the coffee table, all the right cushions...

Tell a childless person that you like having your quiet time awake in the night and you will be stared at with incomprehension. I was that childless person once. A friend had a baby when we were all still at uni. I'm ashamed to say we drifted apart because I couldn't understand her world at all. I understand *now*, if that's worth anything, now that I have a baby of my own to tune into — and more in tune I am because of it! I think, at the time, we abstractly believed she was struggling but, looking back, she was actually doing an amazing job. And, like me, she had loving support from her husband. Her friends didn't treat her as well as they should have done, but a twenty-year-old undergraduate had stepped up to the challenge of motherhood and not been found wanting. I remember once shouting at Jason for treating her like an invalid, insensible to the idea that he was actually supporting her and that my subjectivity counted for nothing. I will try harder to understand about other people's lives now. I will. After all, I need them to understand about mine!

Change sides. I think I'd like to go back to bed. I'm a bit cold now, my feet are, anyway. I should have put on some socks. I try tucking up one foot under my other leg to keep it warm. This makes Hal pop off but, to my delight, he finds my breast again and carries on feeding. I am so impressed with this that I wake up a bit, plan how I will tell Daddy about it in the morning. He'll be pleased for me in his encouraging way, although he is less interested in the minutiae now he knows I'm getting the hang of this. I hope I'm getting the hang of this. Hal's gone to sleep with his mouth full and I'm worried he's going to wake up again. Holding him close, I stand up carefully, the cushions fall to the floor and I step over them carefully and we make our way upstairs. Down Hal goes, into his basket. Will he stay asleep? He's had two sides, well nearly, a side and a bit, was that like last night? Does this mean we're in a routine? That I will not tell Daddy in the morning — he always teases me for thinking that something happening twice constitutes a pattern! I get my sewing and sit on the stairs while I wait to see how settled my little boy is. I wake up in a silent house with my head on my chest.

The Moses basket is in the way and I have to crawl up from the foot of the bed. My side of the bed is cold now but I need to get warm. My human hot water bottle, dear Jase, is over on his side. I put my arm round him and cuddle up to his back. Things are different now, closeness comes in a new way; this moment is precious when our time awake is so busy. I believe him when he tells me that he cuddles me when he gets into bed. I go first ('up you go, sleeping minutes girl') and he follows at midnight or so. You're lovely, you are. We have this wonderful baby. There he is, in his basket. I don't know how to thank you. I press a kiss on the back of your neck. In between my two amazing, magical boys, peaceful sleep finally comes to me.

CHARLOTTE BUCHANAN

This piece is dedicated to the amazingly supportive friends from those early days of motherhood: all at the Ellen Brown Breastfeeding Café in Bermondsey and LLL Bromley. And of course, to Jason.

Photograph by Emma Gates

Daddy's Eyes — a Forces Lullaby

Hush sweet darling, beautiful baby,
Lying, crying on Mamma's knee.
I'll whisper you secrets my beautiful angel;
Daddy loves you from overseas,
Daddy sees you, hears you, nears you.
Your Daddy's eyes smile up, now, at me.

Hush sweet baby, darling of ours
Your Daddy is missing you, sad from afar,
But while he is lonely and I hug you only
Keep your Daddy's eyes all afire on my knee
Keep your Daddy's eyes all afire on my knee.

Softly, softly we'll dream you and me
Of a day not far off now, we'll again be "we three".

LUCY HOLMES

The Father of My Children

The father of my children
Provider and Protector
Cherisher of his family
There to lean on, my wall

Dependable, predictable
No surprises but that's okay
Bringing light to dark moments
Recovering me from my storms

The supporting line of our square
Bearing all the heavy load
The father of my children
Cherish you more than I can show

BENAIFER BHANDARI

Bread

Since becoming a father, I find my mental processes are not quite as sharp as I half-remember them being. One night I was looking after our little boy while my wife Katie was online. I fancied some toast. The train of thoughts that followed seemed to summarize the happy mental fog of domesticity in which I nowadays live.

Hmm, I want some toast. Where's the bread?

Hmm. Can't find the bread. Perhaps it's in the bread bin?

Empty.

It's never in the bread bin.

Why do we have a bread bin? It's always empty.

I'm going to put that bread bin away in the garage.

One day.

Perhaps the bread's in the fridge?

No. But there is a sandwich.

Katie must have made it for my lunch tomorrow.

And used up all the bread.

Hmm. She didn't get a new loaf out of the freezer though.

That's not like her.

Where's the baby?!

Argh! Almost in the cat food...

Gotcha!

Crazy boy.

Right, where's the bread?

Perhaps I should ask Katie?

Yeah, because she's probably hidden the bread, and would really appreciate me coming to disturb her moment of peace.

Oh for goodness sake, stop wriggling. I'm putting you down, all right?

Okay. I need new bread.

Urgh. I hate it when the bread is frozen. It always breaks in the middle because I'm too impatient when I prise the slices apart.

I should get a spatula or something.

Nah, I'm sure it'll be fine this time.

Whoops.

Oh, well. It'll taste the same.

Right. Into the toaster.

Hmm. What shall I have on it?

Jam?

Marmite?

Hmm.

Where's the baby?!

Argh! Halfway up the stool and making for the toaster.

Gotcha!

Crazy boy.

Okay. Butter. Where's the butter?

Ah! There it is, on the table.

By the bread.

TOMAS CYNRIC

Two Become Three

Once we were two
now we are three
how easy it is to forget
what to do.
Time runs away
from our over-filled hourglass
never to be returned
leaving us grasping
at grains of sand.
Now we are three
and happy so to be
fulfilled and in turn hands
that held each other
hold the tiny hands of another.
So perfectly formed
so beautifully waved
that first time at six weeks.
Now she has a regal wrist.
Our girl is growing strong
while we two must be strong
to contain the emotions
that two became three unleashed.
Confusion and happiness,
tiredness mixed with delight,
fear with wonderment,
beauty and desire.
For each fresh day
what will it bring
into our lives with
our child? We do not know
but reach out and embrace it
with three pairs of arms.

JIM DAWSON

Tracy, Shaun & Teyla
Photograph by Lisa Scott: www.lisascottphotography.com
Reproduced by permission of Rosie Evans

Sleeping
Doodle by Angie Stevens

Everyday Life

●●●

Thursday Morning 11 a.m.

Wind blowing
Birds singing
Cars passing.

You and I
Curled together
Milky napping.

Phone ringing
Eyelids flickering
Stroking head
Sleep returning.

Thursday morning 11 a.m.

KIRSTEN FOUBISTER

On the Carpet

The heat of the chilli, the cumin, the take away nights,
the wine poured sparkling in the glowing firelight.

And this carpet — lived in, loved on, worn out — the canvas of life
where every speck, each smudge, those stains, hold a story

Of love and birth and life, of chamomile nights, of days
of coffee, of matchstick eyes, of milky leaks and nappy delights.

ALISON LOCK

Christabel & Zachary
Photograph by Lisa Scott: www.lisascottphotography.com
Reproduced by permission of Rosie Evans

Four a.m. feed

Beyond the window
Apple boughs sigh, frame a moon
Circled in ice. Frost
Whitens a pond, but here all
Is warmth, a cocoon of peace.

PAULINE KIRK

Jude breastfeeding outlined
Image by Alex Florschutz

High Heels and Lipstick

Clickety-clack, clickety-clack. Must be ten o'clock, there goes Carol from up the road in her high heels, lipstick bright, hair neat, covers on the pram spotless. I twitch the curtain so she can't see me — still in my dressing-gown, hair all over the place, house covered in laundry — and sit on the stairs to feed the baby... again.

How does she do it? Why can't I be like that — organized? Am I "coping"? Doesn't feel like it. Sometimes it's blissful, when the baby relaxes in my arms and falls asleep at the breast. Often it's stressful — when she screams and I can't understand why and don't know what to do about it...

***

Somehow, we got through those days, and nights, and sometimes I even made it out of the front door — to an LLL meeting on good days! (I was always late, but they didn't seem to mind).

Years later I met Carol at work, when our children were teenagers. With a wry smile, I told her how I'd been so impressed by her, all those years ago. She chuckled and said, 'That's the only way I could stay halfway sane! I was falling to bits at home, I just had to get out of the door, and the high heels and lipstick were to make me feel as if I was "coping" when I wasn't at all!'

I wish I'd known; we could have had a laugh about it when we needed to. I wish I hadn't assumed I was the only one drowning in isolation. I wish I'd got to know her better, and allowed her to know me with all my failings. I wish women could help each other more and compete less.

RACHEL O'LEARY

76

Emma and Josiah
Photograph by Lisa Scott: www.lisascottphotography.com
Reproduced by permission of Rosie Evans

Love Potion

'Ah, now just look at that —
Sleeping, is he? That's the stuff.'
The old man bends down
with toothless grin:
'I wondered how you stopped that din.'
I pull my baby close,
and nod at him.
A shy smile lets me keep
a mother's age-old secret;
Little does the old chap know
what leaves him so impressed:
I'm feeding my baby at my breast.

ALISON PARKES

78

Nursing and Babywearing

Soft folds of wrapped fabric
    gently caress his tender skin
as baby sleeps, tucked
    close to mama's breast.
Baby wakes, he nestles
    closer as mama
moves about, carrying her
    precious little one —
        ...close to her heart, and
        close at hand.

BETSY FINN

The Answer I Keep in My Heart

'Oh', has been the frequent response, usually paired with a look of borderline dislike, following my answer to the question, 'Why are you still breastfeeding your son?' Sigh. As a passionate breastfeeding mom, it can be so frustrating to know what to say when asked this sensitive question. It is particularly hard to answer, especially when the question is paired with that look. If you have or are currently breastfeeding, you know the look. The look only a nursing mom can get from a non-supportive person.

So, what is my answer? I guess I could tell them that it is still so nutritionally sound for my fourteen-month-old, and how it decreases my chances of ever getting breast cancer. Or maybe I could really shock them, by going into detail about the overwhelming early weeks. That they were filled with engorgement, severe thrush for weeks on end, or the fleeting moments where I could have given up, and how after that kind of commitment, I deserve to breastfeed for as long as I want to. But no, that's just not the way I would go about it. The following words are that which I would truly love to say...

'Calm. Stillness. A feeling of peace. This is what we all strive to feel, if even for a moment. This is what breastfeeding brings for me. For some people, it could be a quiet morning with coffee in hand, sitting on a porch watching a beautiful sunrise. For a golf lover, maybe an early morning tee off, during that quiet and peaceful moment, right before the ball goes airborne. For a pet lover, having a furry, four-legged friend curled up sleeping in their lap, as they read a book. For others, it could be a much-needed meditation followed up with yoga. But for me... it is watching my baby latch on to my beautiful healthy breast, and experiencing a bond in the most natural way I can ever imagine.

'Sometimes the moments leading up to it aren't so calm. At times, they are filled with tears, frustration or tumbles on wobbly legs. But the moment we curl up in our favourite chair, and he latches on while I kiss his little feet, there is such a beautiful stillness, a mutual calm, a feeling that is so full of love that it moves me to tears. To me, it is staying in the moment, and enjoying every second. Because for me, one day this beautiful journey will have to end. But for you, my friend, there will always be a new sunrise, a round of golf, a pet to cuddle, or a time in your day for yoga. But for me, and it fills me with a great sadness to say, my passion wasn't meant to last forever. But oh, I so wish it could. So I will hold my baby and I will comfort him with my breast, I will snuggle him, and I will nurse him for as long as this path allows me to take.'

So, there is my answer to the much-dreaded question. But that answer I will keep in my heart, and instead, I will simply reply with this one, 'Because I still can'.

CINDI EASTMAN

The Softest Place on Earth
Photograph by Alex Simon

Milking Demonstration

We stack children on straw bales,
watch the farm hand sculpt arcs
of milk. My toddler son stares.

'Look Mummy! What...' 'Later,'
I hush his fast-flowing questions.

The cow ignores us; unchurned
by her white, tin-pailed tune.

We move onto the pigpen.
Umpteen snouts nudge and nuzzle
a luxuriant sow, guzzle her warmth.

'Look Mummy, look!' I mime a smile
at his fast-growing world. Too fast.

Already my unnursed breasts tingle,
sting with memory's let-down.

SARAH JAMES

Kids

A mother's milk in two strong jets
lands in the pail beside the steps.
My mother's hands caress each teat
and bring forth liquids warm and sweet,
as white as snow, and just as wet.

A lucky kid who knew no threat
and never will repay the debt
of gifts now nearly obsolete
a mother's milk.

We never had a telly set
but kept two goats (more friends than pets)
and their two kids like me replete
with all they'd need to be complete.
So full of praise let's not forget
a mother's milk.

BEN JOHNSON

A Modern Madonna

No fragile female this
no Ad-man's dream of youth and cream.
This Madonna wears overalls.
She has learnt skills modern saints require
like cleaning floors, unblocking drains.

Somewhere up North, her Joe is working
or joking among a smirk of reps.
Mary understands their case:
the nuclear family with father itinerant.
A lifetime ago she studied Politics

Got two A's and a B.
Gabriel changed all that.
Now she nurses a sleepy child,
while the TV reminds: 'Eight
shopping days to Christmas.'

As if she could forget!
Above 'Jingle bells' and 'Rudolph'
she catches a strain of angel song,
but the shepherds are stuck in traffic.
Smiling to camera, she waits for Joe
and asks the Magi in for tea.

PAULINE KIRK

The Statue of Our Lady
A stone statue by an unknown sculptor — originally from France —
which resides in the Catholic Church of Our Lady, Star of the Sea, on
Tobermory, Isle of Mull, Scotland.
Photograph by Lisa Hassan Scott

85

Diary of a Wimpy Toddler-Feeding Mum

January. Late morning. Snow!
Nowhere to be... so back to bed we go.
Mummy's milk, a story. Another one. A few!
A back and tummy tickle then napping until two.

Sunday. Guests. Table and roast.
Wine for the rabble but water for the host.
Pouring gravy with one hand, holding daughter with the other.
She chews me. I chew the fat. I am a super mother!

Midweek. Dead of night. Oh! No! Awake.
Cow-heavy, tired. I lie and grumble-ache.
Sucking on the left, squeezing on the right;
Does she *really* need to pinch and suckle through the night?

Hot. The Underground. Sweating pits and brow.
Thirsty daughter pulling blouse. I whisper, '*Please!* Not *now!*'
Pick her up and snuggle her close in to my chest.
Lady opposite smiles at me, so frankly — sod the rest!

May. Lunchtime. Busy department store.
Tired and angry toddler sprawled across the floor.
Whoops. Bad timing. Scoop my breast out fast.
Remonstrating glances from the shoppers walking past.

Summer's day. The Playground. Picnic for her tea.
Kamikaze-head-first down the slide comes she.
A revving engine startles her. Suddenly she's here,
For a little bit of num num to allay her fear.

Twilight. After bath. My favourite time of day.
Upstairs to my bedroom, it's time to "hit the hay"
Hairbrushed and pink-pyjamaed, I lay her down to rest.
Her blanket is my dressing gown, her pillow is my breast.

Darkness. Stillness. She's let go into sleep,
But my eyes fast upon my daughter's face I keep.
I love this moment most of all. In trance I guard her rest.
It's here beside her on the bed that I feel truly blessed.

Drat! Lunch with the in-laws. Must try to keep them in.
Wear high-roll, buttoned polo neck to cover up my skin.
During tea, she lunges, the polo neck's rolled up.
Aghast, my in-law father splutters shortbread in his cup.

September. Friday. School assembly hall.
Surreptitious feeding underneath my shawl
I hate myself for sneaking. I feel pathetic. Weak.
Why can't I proudly breastfeed without feeling like a *freak?*

November. Her birthday. Another threshold. Three!
At times with toddler feeding, I have felt lost at sea.
It's mostly done at home now — after nursery, before bed.
But we still sleep together; nose to nose and head to head.

End of year. Close of poem. Breastfeeding yet to cease.
I trust her need and know my heart, and that's what brings me peace.

NADIA RAAFAT

The Cold Cup of Tea

An already-cold cup of builder's-strength tea
Is sat by the sink, and saying to me:
'I'm delicious, delightful, so drink me up, do!'
But I'm knee-deep in nappies, and children, and poo;
So call me again when I've sorted this mess
And have time to relax, and unwind and de-stress...

*

Later, much later, when the kids are asleep,
In my nightie and slippers I quietly creep
To the kitchen, and there is that cold cup of tea,
Still delicious, still delightful, and still waiting for me...

MARIJA SMITS

Happy Birthday!

Birth
day
begins
like any other day
till happy boy
full of smiles
plunges across sleepy pillows,
in his hands and eyes
a Gift,
cherished
beneath his pillow
through the night.
Crumpled card
brimming with flowers,
red, purple, blue,
bursts with love.
Baby brother
beams,
tears paper
from presents
meant for mum.
Hugs, kisses,
while lover, husband, friend
looks on, smiling,
remembering
other
Birth
Days.

ALISON PARKES

Reflections on Returning to Work...

When asked about my thoughts on returning to work following a period of maternity leave I didn't know how to begin; one thought, however, that persisted through a myriad of emotions was that I would much rather stay at home to look after my children. I felt like I was giving them up!

I found myself asking what was I most concerned about and for whom was I concerned? Surely in times such as these with an abundance of childcare resources, largely set up to enable parents like me to return to work after having a baby, it should all feel easy and manageable. I shouldn't feel concerned or even guilty about having to return to work. But that is exactly how I felt for reasons which gradually became clearer to me.

I had begun to feel separation anxiety even before returning to work. I used to think that this is what babies and young children experience when separated from a parent, but here was I, an adult, experiencing it in reverse direction. When my nine-month-old daughter was undergoing her settling in period at nursery only just very recently, I would wait in Starbucks before collecting her, feeling emotional and teary-eyed as I found myself surrounded by other mums who had their babies with them while I longed for mine. It all felt so wrong to me. I had never felt anything quite like this on returning to work following my first and second child so why was I feeling less enthusiastic about returning to paid work after my third child? What was different this time?

I think the answer lies in the realization that I have had such an enriching mothering experience this time round that I don't want to let go of it for fear I might not experience it again. I have enjoyed it all the more because looking after a baby has become easier following all that I learnt from having two other children. I have enjoyed seeing my baby interact with her two older siblings from a very young age and I recognize how they, in turn, have contributed to her development. I have enjoyed the social and supportive aspects of attending La Leche League meetings, becoming a member of LLL, attending activities run by local childcare centres and other mother and child focussed services. All of this has required time and plenty of it, and now I don't have this kind of time any more.

Above all, I have learnt to recognize the value of being a mother at home, by being there for my children to enable them to feel secure, happy and loved in their day-to-day lives. It doesn't mean that my children can't or won't feel happy now that I've returned to work, but the important job of mothering seems all the more hard when trying to condense it into the beginning and end of each working day. I can only be grateful for the fact that my children don't tire as easily as I do and, as always, are very accepting of their mother and the varying amount of time we spend together.

EMER MARTIN

Homecoming

It's been a hard night's day
and I've been working.
Yes, working.
Trapped in a world of
deadlines and meetings,
and meeting deadlines,
surreal after baby-broken nights.

The world of work
allows my mind to leave behind
the baby
left abruptly
with a friend (who cares for him)
amid the chaos of another start
to another day.
Grown-up talk, adult banter,
sedate
my hormonal and emotional state.
Like an illicit lover,
I force him from my thoughts;
though the memory
of his downy head upon her shoulder
delivers the occasional shaft
of pain.

Now it is the rushing hour
to home
and him.
Milk swelling in my breasts
strains buttons and decorum.
In the solitude of my car
I allow my aching heart
time to ache
and step dangerously on the accelerator.
Then with little grace

he is flung from house to car to home.
Only when the door slams
behind us
can we both yield to the primitive
urge of both mother and baby:
to be together.

His tossing head searches frantically for my milk,
and for me.
I press his taut little body
tight against mine,
and feel with relief the milk begin to flow.
Blessed peace washes over us both.

In my arms I watch him at my breast:
his funny little frown of concentration,
the way he strokes my finger with his tiny thumb.
I caress the heavenly softness of his tummy,
relearning
the feel of him, the smell of him,
and tuck his soft head beneath my chin.

And when at last, replete,
his eyelids close,
his milky lips part,
and his rosy face glows
with satisfaction,
his body sags into sleep.
I hold him —
and the moment —
close to my heart.
For this is when I know
I have truly come home.

ALISON PARKES

Mother and others
Painting by Jo Welch

Challenging Times

•••

Warriors of Love

Mothers are wonderful warriors,
We are warriors of love.
We risk everything, everyday:
Our own connection to ourselves, our inner peace,
Our joy and our hope.
To commit to another this fully is to be brave beyond measure
For we cannot choose what will happen
And may lose everything in an instant.

ANNA MORTON

95

Twice as Nice? My Tandem Nursing Journey

I was definitely going to breastfeed for the recommended six months. Possibly even for a year. That was assuming that it all worked out okay, which it might not. Many, many people made a point of telling me that it might not work out. That they didn't or couldn't breastfeed successfully. That I shouldn't be disappointed if I didn't manage more than a few weeks.

At the time of writing, I've been breastfeeding for two years and ten months. And for the last eight of those months I've been tandem feeding. If you took me back in time to my pre-baby days, my early baby days, and told me that one day I'd write the two sentences that start this paragraph I'd have thought you were crazy. Back then, I had never heard of tandem feeding. It didn't occur to me that someone would do such a thing. Twins, yes. Children of different ages? Never crossed my mind.

So, how did I come to be a 24-7 milk bar to my two minis?

I just didn't get around to weaning. I didn't see the need to wean. I didn't *feel* the need to wean, not even when bemused friends asked me if I was still breastfeeding. Always with the emphasis on "still".

I had an occasional vague thought about weaning, but truthfully, I'm kind of lazy about that sort of stuff and it seemed to me like weaning from the breast would entail a lot of hard work and involve a lot of tears (for both of us). And anyway, I liked it — loved it, even. I loved the closeness, the cuddliness, the warmth. I loved the fact that I could always make my daughter feel better, physically and emotionally. I loved the fact that when she was teething, or poorly, she was still getting plenty of nutritional fluids from me. I particularly loved how it helped her to sleep. Breastfeeding was a huge part of our relationship. It was a huge part of who I was as a mother. I was only half joking when I told people that I was planning to add "breastfeeding" to my CV under "Hobbies and Interests".

I found out I was pregnant when my daughter was around eighteen months old. The pregnancy was planned. I'd carefully looked into whether it was possible to conceive during breastfeeding (it is) and whether breastfeeding would endanger my foetus in anyway (it didn't). I dreaded feeding through the "sore nipple" phase, but figured I could grit my teeth for those few weeks. And many, many sources told me that my daughter would most probably wean during pregnancy, as this was extremely common. I'm a firm believer in child-led development, so that seemed like the ideal solution. She would wean herself. Everyone said so.

Never underestimate the tenacity of a boob-addicted toddler. Even when the nectar dried up at around the sixth or seventh month, she valiantly kept sucking away. My research into feeding during pregnancy had prepared me for the possibility of my milk drying up (even though I didn't really believe that it would, for some reason), but I had no inkling about gestational nursing aversion. Breastfeeding had been one of the most essential aspects of our mother-daughter dyad. Now, I hated it so much I had to grit my teeth and count slowly to twenty to stop myself from picking her up and flinging her across the room. Whereas once I'd adored holding her close and holding her soul-deep gaze as we nursed, now all I wanted was to get her as far away from my breasts as possible. I felt like the most hateful mother in the world. I wrestled with this for a long time. It kept me awake at night. Had I stopped loving my daughter as much now that I had another baby on the way? Was she aware of how I felt, on some level, and if so would she remember this rejection, feel hurt or scared by it? Would she carry these emotional scars with her, and would they turn her against her sibling when it made its way into the world?

Thankfully — and quite by chance — I stumbled upon a fellow sufferer's account of nursing aversion on a natural parenting forum, and this lead me to other resources which reassured me that this was a natural hormonal response. Apparently it is very common for pregnant mammals to experience feelings of aggression towards their nursing young. Knowing this didn't make the feelings go away, but it did make them easier to tolerate. Knowing that I was not abnormal (or, at least, no more "abnormal" than any other pregnant nursing mother in our early-weaning, pro-formula Western culture!) I continued to grit my teeth and counted down the days until my baby — and therefore my new supply of milk — arrived.

Daughter number two arrived when her big sister was twenty-six months old, and with the birth of my second girl, a tandem-nursing mother was also born.

It would be easier second time around, right? I knew what to expect, I was nothing if not well-practised in this womanly art of breastfeeding. Our nursing dyad would seamlessly become a triad.

What could be more simple, more natural? True, I didn't know exactly what to expect; I hadn't come across much about tandem nursing (maybe I hadn't looked for much on tandem nursing: I was — naively — expecting more of the same) and based upon the little that I did find, I looked forward to a Gaia-esque experience of total contentment and beatific maternal calm.

To say that it has been tough is putting it mildly.

Instead of becoming the warm and milky focus of sibling bonding and affectionate harmony, I often felt that I was being pulled in two directions at once, emotionally as well as physically. I didn't want my older girl to feel that she had been usurped, pushed aside, or that her needs were irrelevant. Yet at the same time I was aware that as well as her essential nutritional needs, my new baby had an equal right to form the same breastfeeding closeness as her sister had been able to do. I was tired from the pregnancy, I was tired from the birth (and the three days of slow labour which had preceded it) and now I was exhausted from juggling the demands of a newborn with trying to reassure my toddler that she was still as important to me as she had always been, and all of this whilst trying to remain true to my attachment parenting philosophy.

It is not unusual for a toddler to increase their nursing when the new baby arrives. The return of your milk supply, a hefty dose of sibling rivalry, and the ever-present sight of you feeding the new arrival are just too tempting for a person that has yet to master the concept of delayed gratification. I liken it to someone putting a huge cake in front of me, after several months of "cake drought", and then telling me that I must stand by and watch someone else — someone who has just arrived — eat it all. So yep, she increased her feedings. Increased them to the point where she was feeding more than the baby. Even the gentlest of deferrals was met with a meltdown, and so I tried my best to flow with it and meet her needs whilst simultaneously meeting the needs of the baby and trying not to completely lose myself at the same time.

It's the toughest thing I've ever done, and I'm sure that one day I'll be incredibly proud of my achievement, although right now, while I am slap bang in the middle of it, it feels not so much like accomplishment as simply being "a thing that I do", like changing nappies and giving cuddles.

Sometimes, on a bad day, it seems like the stupidest decision I ever made. But then the alternative was parent-led weaning, and I've always aimed towards child-led parenting. Sometimes I still do the slow counting, focussing on the corner of the room, the top of the curtains, the dappled pattern of the sun on the carpet — anything to keep my mind elsewhere and allow the seconds to tick past.

And then sometimes, when I look down to see my girls smiling at each other, or holding hands across me, or when my toddler asks (in her sweetest voice, and with her cutest face) 'Please can we share some, mummy?', then my heart swells, and I'm glad that we get to share this rare closeness, a closeness that I hope will not only be an intrinsic part of my relationship with each of my girls, but will also help to build an unshakeable closeness between them too.

HELEN COOPER

When My Baby was Unwell

My sweet, sad boy
huge doe eyes
in a drawn, pale face.
How my heart
wants to wrap itself around you
and snuggle you in close,
keep you safe and make you well.
How patient you are
how gentle
how loving
shocked, weak and quiet.
Yet your curiosity
can still be lit
like a spark
but slowly, more softly
than usual.
Brown eyes full of trust
they look at me
with and without questions.
And all I can answer
is Yes, Yes, Yes
I love you and I want to help you
sweet, sweet
darling boy.

LISA KATZ

A Wonderful Thing

Nothing has fulfilled me in quite such a beautiful way as becoming a mother and experiencing the daily love, depths of feeling (high and low), and joy that it brings. Breastfeeding was an exquisite experience in which I felt the bliss of nurturing my babies; an expression of the love I was feeling. Indeed it was a wonderful thing that I knew I *could* do in my helpless state to comfort them and assist their recovery when they were unwell.

LISA KATZ

Eye 2
Photograph by Alex Florschutz

Tears in Her Eyes

Let me set the scene: You are in a shopping mall, running a stall in aid of breastfeeding awareness week. Lots of different people come by, some stop and chat, others just rush by.

Women tell you: 'Oh – I have done that.'

'Breastfeeding didn't work for me.'

'Breastfeeding never was an option.'

'I am still doing it.'

I think you get my drift...

And then all of a sudden — out of the blue, a mother screams at you: 'It is not that easy or simple' and tears are standing in her eyes. Baffled you try to talk to her, try to explain that you didn't mean to hurt her; that you know how complicated breastfeeding sometimes is. But she doesn't stop, she nearly runs away from you; leaving you with a sense of sadness and bewilderment.

Where did this come from? Why is this woman still reeling with the emotions from her breastfeeding times after so many years?

This is just one of several encounters I have had with women who, even years later, were still hurting from the experience and the resulting feeling of failure.

I couldn't let go of these encounters without a satisfactory explanation. I went down many different roads, but all of them left me with the feeling that I was missing something, that the explanations were good, but not covering everything.

***

Until one day I had to put a presentation about breastfeeding together and I had ten minutes to make my point. I decided to find one statement that encapsulates the most important point for me. Easier said than done...

I went through the benefits, but that would fill pages. So I started with the reasons behind the breastfeeding. Why do women want to breastfeed? And that's when it hit me. The whole time I had been putting breastfeeding into the wrong framework. I had looked at it from these different perspectives:

- Mother-baby relationship
- Family
- The community
- Our society.

All these frameworks were right and they were also not enough. The reason why women want to breastfeed comes from an evolutionary point of view. Everything we do (eating, sleeping etc.) is designed with one view in mind:

That we as human beings survive.

Nature didn't know that we would live in heated houses, be able to buy food and have blankets to keep our babies warm — or to put it from a different perspective: nature has designed life in a way that it relies as much as it can on the human being and very little on things; all these survival mechanisms run on instincts.

The baby's instincts make it to want to stay with a source of warmth (physical and emotional) and food (often the mother) as it would otherwise not survive.

We, as women, get hit during our pregnancy with the first connection, or reawakening, of our instincts and when the baby is born we get hit by another dose. Every woman will experience this, with varying degrees, but it will be there.

The reaction to it will be culturally (societally) shaped and again vary a lot. But at the end of the day — when it comes to breastfeeding — our bodies and minds are run by our instincts.

Therefore if a woman, for whatever reason, doesn't succeed in breastfeeding her baby, the sense of loss and failure goes much deeper than intellect or emotions; it connects on an instinctual level. This woman has "failed" the human race as she hasn't been able to do the most basic thing: to feed her baby.

This sense of failure goes much deeper than any other failure someone experiences in their life.

There is very little grasp on this in our society, as most people will approach it from a logical viewpoint and say: 'Well you did your best, it just didn't work out', or 'You had to give a bottle — you didn't want your baby to starve', or 'What is your problem? You are still feeding your baby. You are just using a bottle.'

These well-meaning replies will work on some level for some women, or at least soothe some of the pain, but don't meet the woman at the root of her deep hurt.

As there are alternative feeding methods there is little understanding that the pain and sorrow is only partly about the sort of food the baby gets and therefore our society then denies these women the right to grieve for their loss.

What these women need is time and space to grieve, debrief and an explanation that meets them on all levels.

So — next time you meet a woman who is very deeply hurt, see if you can give her some of what she has been missing and help her to put it in the bigger framework.

Maybe the ability to understand and be understood can then be the first step to heal.

PETRA HOEHFURTNER

From a Dark Place to Acceptance

My experiences with my two children have been so different. With my first, it seemed that everything worked against me getting breastfeeding off to a good start. And I didn't know to ask for the support I needed and couldn't overcome the challenges. Breastfeeding very quickly ground to a halt and my son ended up being bottle-fed. At the time, I actually felt relieved about this. I was depressed and in a very dark place. Breastfeeding was all part of the sense of being utterly overwhelmed and pressured at becoming a mother, and making the decision initially to stop breastfeeding and then gradually to stop expressing (I stopped at nine weeks) was part of me trying to gain some sense of normality over the situation.

However, now looking back it makes me deeply sad — I know how much I missed out on with him and how the system failed us both. I also realize that not breastfeeding him probably contributed to my depression because it went against what my body and mind expected.

When I was pregnant with my daughter, I found out lots more and got the right support, and even with some struggles in the early days, breastfeeding has worked really well for us. I have loved breastfeeding — it's been so much more than just food. It's an easy way to connect with, calm and enjoy my daughter. It's one of my proudest achievements. And it's been much less tiring and hard work than bottle-feeding. For me, the big difference second time round was getting the right support from the right people (my local La Leche League group) and I'm very thankful to them!

I love both my children the same; I would do anything for either of them. But when I look back at the early months and years, there is a difference. With my bottle-fed son, I felt like a mother loving and looking after this wonderful, gorgeous baby, but we were separate people and I had to work out how to get to know him and understand him. With my breastfed daughter, it felt like much more of a partnership — like there was a synergy between us and that there was just this implicit understanding that we were in sync.

Someone once asked me if I had noticed a difference in attitudes to the different ways I have fed my children, and it saddens me to say that I have felt more judged, pressured and uncomfortable as a breastfeeding mum than I ever did as a bottle-feeding mum. I wouldn't have thought twice about feeding my son in a café with a bottle, whereas I would always feel some degree of self-consciousness when breastfeeding my daughter. I always found bottle-feeding to be more "acceptable" in society and to provoke less judgement than breastfeeding.

I now hang out with people who understand, and that continues to make all the difference to me.

RACHEL ASHE

More

Baby Boy you deserve more.
More than mummy can give.
I want to give you more.
More love
more time
more attention
more of me.
Baby Boy you deserve more
more smiles
more hugs
more enjoyment
more of that from me.
I want to give you more
I want to enjoy you more
love you more
hug, smile and see you more.
That is why I'm taking this pill.
You are my battle cry because
the fight goes on
and you deserve more.

LUCY BENTON

Mothering Ethan

My breastfeeding journey didn't begin as I thought it would. Right after my son, Ethan, was born we had thirty minutes of skin-to-skin contact, and he latched on to my breast like a pro. But he stopped breathing whilst still nestled on my chest. High on my bliss, I failed to notice. Thank goodness for my eagle-eyed midwife. He was resuscitated and sent up to the neonatal unit.

I spent two days on the ward without him, trying to heal from the emergency caesarean I had undergone. I became obsessed with trying to assuage my feelings of guilt for not having had a natural birth, so I preoccupied myself with trying to express some colostrum. But what with our separation and the emotional upheaval, I found this difficult to do. I used a breast pump and spent time stimulating my breasts to produce milk.

Thankfully, I did go up and have Ethan suckle. That was one move that actually helped. Feeling uncomfortable with the lack of empathy and privacy on the ward, I was much happier when we got home. My milk arrived the next day, and I was so glad that at last I could do this one thing for my child: I could breastfeed him.

***

Becoming a mother has unearthed a lot for me. It has made me look at my own childhood — the highs and the lows. When Ethan was eight months old I was diagnosed with postnatal depression. I was almost relieved that the feelings I was experiencing could be named and that I could begin medication. Two months on, I'm still living with postnatal depression, but recovering daily.

In spite of Ethan's reflux and lactose intolerance, I see him growing and thriving. Mother's milk has been healing for both of us. It has been gentle on Ethan's maturing gut and kept us bonded even through my postnatal depression. Having nurtured him thus far makes me know that we'll be okay.

LUCY BENTON

One Day at a Time

The snow on the mountainside was glittering from the afternoon sunlight, and below us was a white sea of clouds that covered most of the valley leaving only the projecting mountain peaks to form a magnificent panorama. I enjoyed the idyllic moment of being together with my family in a beautiful place. My nausea and dizziness were bound to return later, after we got back to the chalet — I knew that and was in no hurry. Instead, I concentrated on the feeling of the moment and took wonder at the brilliant white snow under a brilliant blue sky.

'We really ski well together,' I thought, 'each of us senses exactly where the others are.' That was reassuring and I felt quiet contentment radiating within me. The unspoken questions were still there, but I ignored them, 'What exactly am I ill with? How ill am I? Is it curable? How can I be there for my family in spite of everything?' All I knew was that movement and sunshine made me feel better, and while I was skiing, I could still mother and support my children.

Over the last few months I have been finding out how much I must have been doing as a mother when I was not ill. These days, I find it hard to stand long enough to cook a meal, and on a bad day, to find the energy to walk to the local store, some ten minutes away. Before... oh it seems such a long time ago, I would happily work online starting from our kids' bedtime until midnight and then contentedly sort the laundry before I went to bed. And before that, way back when the kids were really small, I would always be on the go with my trusty over-the-shoulder sling, lulling the little ones to sleep with my movement, and nurturing them with my milk, providing warmth and comfort by being close. In retrospect it seems easy. Easier than this, anyhow.

We had become new parents in a country where we had no family. We also knew nobody with small children. We were fortunate, though, that my mother would travel long distances to help us whenever she could — her kind and gentle presence was very uplifting and comforting. I joined La Leche League and found the support of other mothers who were breastfeeding, like me, and our conversations united us somehow. I do not remember feeling hindered or judged because of breastfeeding or any of the other lifestyle choices that we made. We had a family bed, I tandem nursed my children, we coped with the usual childhood illnesses, and night terrors and pneumonia. We got to know our children well and we taught them what we could and whenever we could — I do not mean formal teaching, but rather the kind of lessons that come naturally. As we live close to the mountains, it was I, and not the ski school, who taught our kids to ski, because the mother in me would not have missed such a delightful opportunity for togetherness and learning.

Going to La Leche League meetings provided me with helpful suggestions and much-needed company in an area where I had almost no friends. This type of company helped me believe in myself and allowed me to dare to make my own path in life.

***

Until last summer I had a rather heavy workload, both at home and at the office, but was coping pretty well, all things considered. However, in June life got much harder. A tick bit me, in spite of my caution. It probably came in on my clothes, and that happened because the school participated in a sports event at the height of the tick season in a tick-ridden forest. No matter about what I could or should have done instead — a tick did bite me and two months later I became ill for the first time.

Then came the fear, 'I am a mother. I cannot be ill. Not like this. Not for so long. What am I going to do?' But because of my mothering experience and the La Leche League meetings I had gone to, I'd already learnt that doctors are people. In spite of their education, experience and reputation, they can also be wrong. They might be overworked, they might be having an off day and not manage to do a diagnosis, or they might misinterpret what you are saying. In most cases, doctors also do not know your lifestyle and how you behave when you are healthy, which makes it difficult for them to see what is normal for you. When it comes to tick-borne diseases, I discovered that many doctors are not tick aware. So I acted upon my own initiative and sent the tick that bit me to a specialized laboratory for analysis to see if it carried any organisms that could cause illness, the two most likely candidates being *Borrelia* (Lyme disease bacteria) and *Rickettsia* (another kind of bacteria). I waited for the results.

In the meantime, I decided to see a specialist for tick-borne diseases, who is a kind man with a lot of experience in his field.

However, some of my first appointments with him left me with the sense that I wasn't being listened to. I was hoping for a definite diagnosis from him, but none was forthcoming. My blood tests for *Borrelia* (Lyme disease bacteria) kept coming back negative, which was of little comfort because false negatives are commonplace, as no precise blood test exists to prove that a patient is **not** infected. The specialist kept telling me that my symptoms were not typical for Lyme disease (*Borreliosis*). Meanwhile I desperately wanted to find out what they were typical for, but they were labelled as "too general".

So I did some surfing on the internet and came across some microbiology journals which are intellectual reading, albeit a bit complicated for somebody like me who has hardly any medical knowledge. I gleaned from them that the symptoms of a tick-borne illness depend strongly on the strain of *Rickettsia* and that, for example, *Rickettsia slovaca* or *Rickettsia helvetica* (which are found all over Europe) do not necessarily cause a fever, and that the medical community does not know much about that illness because there are no routine tests for it. While chatting to people at work, I discovered that the general public is even less aware of tick-borne diseases. Most people do not realize that there is no immunization against Lyme disease (*Borreliosis*).

The breakthrough came when I finally received the results of the tick analysis (the padded envelope that contained the tick had got stuck at the border because I had not filled in the customs declaration, which slowed things down considerably). The lab report said that the tick tested positive for *Borrelia* (Lyme disease bacteria) and *Rickettsia* (bacteria). I presented the results of the tick analysis to the specialist and we agreed that I should get a blood test done for *Rickettsia*. It became apparent that at some point in time I had had *Rickettsiosis* (*Rickettsia* infection). As a new bout of illness was starting, I was given a course of antibiotics. However, doctors were still not sure what I was ill with.

***

My course of antibiotics is long over, and I wish for a happy end. However, at the moment I find myself needing to cope with nerve and muscle twitches, and occasional buzzing in my hands and legs. I get tired easily and need to lie down on the sofa often, something that I never used to do. Then there are the headaches that come just before rain or snow storms, and occasional ringing in my ears. Most days my attitude is fairly positive, but whenever even a bit of vertigo or nausea returns, so does the fear — if *Rickettsiosis* got transmitted to me from the tick, I keep wondering what the chances were of getting *Borreliosis* at the same time. I now keep a symptoms diary and have decided to join a self-help group, because people in a similar situation are most likely facing the same challenges as me and can provide support and information, and *vice versa*. Also, my earlier years spent in mothers' meetings discussing healthy eating are now helping me choose foods that boost my immune system. Spinach has been a particular craving for a while, and I have learned that eating foods high in magnesium helps to combat the muscle twitches.

Meanwhile, music has continued to carry me through tough times. If I have enough energy, I do karaoke with the kids, but mostly I prefer listening to talented singers. Children's books have also kept me company, and I'm glad for poetry. Additionally, I am glad to build igloos because shovelling snow makes me feel better. The specialist says that I need patience, and I guess he is right. So I am taking it one day at a time.

RITA KORNELL

Farewell to my baby

'It is not good news I'm afraid,
There is no movement,
No heart beat.'
No
Heart
Beat
And our hearts break
Snap, like Ella's crocodile.

11 weeks and 2 days
Just over 4 cm
But with eyelids, hair and fingernails.
It is amazing how attached you get to someone you've never met.
Someone you only dreamed.
No
Heart
Beat.

We will never hold you
Never see you smile
Never stroke your hair or
Sing you to sleep.
Not this time.
No
Heart
Beat.

And even though we know
You chose to go to another safe place to wait for another time:
your time
We grieve because that safe place is not with us.
No
Heart
Beat.

We have a picture of the shadow you.
The real you left 3 weeks and 2 days ago.
The night when Ella screamed for hours and we didn't know why.
She knew her little brother was gone.
No
Heart
Beat.

And now we wait for my body to give up yours, your earthy shell,
Which is still tucked within me.
Where it has been for such a long short time.
It is hard to let you go.
No
Heart
Beat.

I watch your sister and I see the way we will heal and accept that your
too short stay was for good reason. I promise.

Goodbye my darling.

Mama

JESSICA STARR

Maternity

One wept whose only child was dead,
New-born, ten years ago.
'Weep not; he is in bliss,' they said.
She answered, 'Even so,

'Ten years ago was born in pain
A child, not now forlorn.
But oh, ten years ago, in vain,
A mother, a mother was born.'

ALICE MEYNELL (1847 — 1922)

To the Stars and the Moon

I never got to meet you,
Little, tiny almost-child;
You slipped away
To the stars and the moon
And didn't come back
To tell Mommy how beautiful they were.

Your big brother
And your not-so-big brother
And your great big Daddy
Were ready to love you;
Ready to let their hearts grow,
Ready to play and tease and wonder
What you thought about them.

So, as I look at the stars and the moon
Could you please let me know
How beautiful they are;
Because sometimes it's hard
For me to see them at all
Without you here to hold my hand.

KATHY GROSSMAN

117

Peace
Painting by Alex Florschutz

When a baby isn't to be

Miscarriage or losing a baby is both a fact and a fear.

If you must leave me, my baby, I thank you.
I let you go with love.
Although for me, I lose you from my flesh, from my body,
from my dreams, I release you.
I know you go back to that place before birth, the one true home,
the place you know.
The place of love.
I release you from my body, from my dreams.
I feel my blood, my tears flow, and I let you go.
But I let you go with love, with blessings.
I thank you for choosing me, as you came down from the stars,
I thank you for using me as your vehicle
for your brief earthly experience.
I hope your brief watery home in my womb was a place of love,
of warmth, of peace.
I hope you felt how wanted you were,
and you learnt that a life here on earth can be a life of love.
Thank you for choosing me, us, our family.
I let you go with love, with blessings.
Back you go to that place beyond places, from where we all began.

Love to you and love to all.

CLARE COOPER

Painting by Jean-Mathieu Wendling

Remembering Mothers

●●●

My Mother

As I breathe; as I am that I am;
I thank you from the very depths
of my heart for being —
for being my mother.

JIM DAWSON

Last Gifts

I have to undo railings to get close,
coax her to take water. My mother
in a cot, sipping a baby's cup.

Face almost hers under the fretted hair.
On hospital bed familiar hands falter.
She has too much to say, and words are rags.

She scans an inch of vision till she finds
my face. My hand between hers, she urges
'I love you very much'.

Eyes swim beyond the waiting room,
no longer knowing me. Ears deaf to my goodbyes.
Only the struggle to breathe, the waiting.

*

Secretly, a girlchild begins
unfolding into grief.

ANGELA TOPPING

Painting by Guy Meynell
Reproduced by permission of the Provost and Fellows of Eton College

Mother's Cardigan

My mother's cardigan
Still hangs on the back of her chair,
A fluffy pink confection
Of kitten-soft mohair,
Crafted by her own hands fair.

Twenty years have come
And gone since she passed on;
But there is not a day,
I do not think of her
Not one that I do not remember,

Close my eyes and visualize
Her needles clacking, glasses slipping
Down her nose,
Brow furrowed, counting rows
Of plain-and-purl stitches.

Tell us a story, we'd say
She'd sigh, toss aside her pattern,
Take off her specs and begin:
'One dark and stormy night
Three robbers went into a cave,

Tell us a story, one said,
So Jack began: One dark and stormy
Night, three robbers went into a cave...'
Not that one, we'd scream.
She couldn't continue for laughing.

In those awful, tearful days
After cancer stole her away,
I would lie quiet on her bed,
Wrap the cardigan around my head
And breathe in the scent of her.

Yardley's Lily of the Valley,
French Fern; the taste of Gardenia.
Gradually, the perfumes slipped away
Like memories fading to sepia.
Often, I forget the garment's still there

Draped over that chair,
Still waiting for her; but I know
I will never forget,
Never stop missing,
Never, ever, stop loving,
My mother.

BOB MUNDELL

Threads

The memories washed, folded and stored
Ironed and teased, hung up and adored
The jumper she wore when we thought she was ill
When she held me and told me she would be there still
The odd shoes we found on confused, weary feet
As she sat in the chair dressed so terribly neat
The nightdress we packed for her one-night stay
But then day turned to night and night turned to day
No more catalogue buying or trips into town
She was dressed for no ball as the nurse tied the gown
The bag we were left with that sits all alone
Don't want to unpack and admit she's not home
Pick out an outfit, must look her best
Shoes have to match as we lay her to rest
Petticoat thoughts drift from the shelf
Remind me that clothes do not make the self
The click of the button that took the snap
That shot through the fabric now leaves a gap
And where did she get those shoes to match?
And why did those jeans end up with a patch?
Her smell, her warmth, zipped into her fashion
A wardrobe of photos that tell of her passion
Her clothes once had life but she's here no more
And all we have left are the threads that she wore

SCOOP

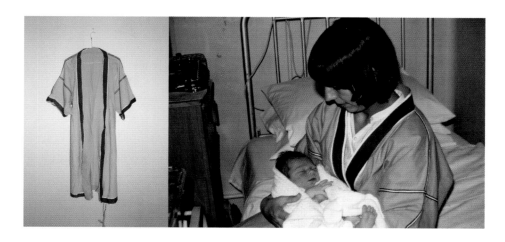

Emma and Christine holding hands on steps, Spain September 1981

Images from *Collecting Christine*
Produced by Emma Gates

From Frailty to Strength and Joy

Dear *Omonim*,[1]

I am writing to you because during that intensely emotional and precious time of our lives when your first granddaughter was born, we could only barely communicate across the vast Anglo-Korean cultural divide.[2] So first of all I want to thank you for your willingness to try and bridge our two cultures, in order to share this experience with me. Thank you for extending your motherly love and wisdom to me, your daughter-in-law.

Looking back, during that first pregnancy, my midwife was concerned that buried grief after having lost my own mother at twenty-one would impact on the experience. I brushed off this theory; as a midwife myself I had supported countless women through the life changing events of giving birth, breastfeeding and becoming a mother. I thought nothing could faze me. I trusted in my professional knowledge and experience and consequently was knocked sideways by the physical strain and passionate emotions of motherhood. You came halfway across the world to be the mother I needed.

Well, at first I didn't want your help at all! You tried to make me rest at the end of the pregnancy but I went the Western way of seeing friends, exercising and "proving my strength" well into those two long weeks past my due date. Then after a straightforward birth, all was rosy for the first few days. Of course I was reluctant to admit I needed to take it easy. I was delighted to welcome our many visitors, while you tried to "rescue" the baby from too many different arms. I was amused when you told me that Korean women stay indoors for *Sanhu jori*, the traditional one hundred days of rest and calm following the birth so that their bones can knit back together.[3] 'We Brits are tougher than that,' I thought. But you were right and I soon began to wear out. You served me *Mi-yok guk* (seaweed soup), the customary Korean remedy for new mothers, to restore blood circulation. You also learned how to make toast and marmalade, and jacket potatoes just as I liked them.

I'm laughing as I remember the "nursing tea" that a friend so kindly gave me. I drank pots and pots. You were vigilant in preparing it: not too hot because you believed very hot or cold drinks would inhibit my body's ability to heal. I started to produce gallons of milk.

Wonderful! Here was more evidence of my natural resilience and the daftness of the notion that I should need help in mothering. However, although the baby took as much as she needed, there was more than she could empty. Engorgement set in and then when I was too blurry with pain and tiredness to sort that out properly I developed mastitis. Ridiculous, I thought, for a midwife. I was so disappointed in myself. But through it all, *Omonim*, you remained serene, never resting, as you nursed me and cared for your granddaughter.

The mastitis recurred and worryingly I was told I needed a breast ultrasound (though it proved unnecessary). Then the compounded lack of sleep overtook me. All this made me feel like such a failure and I resented my dependence on you. You were businesslike, staying on top of the babycare, the housework and urging me to nap, just as I have advised so many new mums in my work: sleep when the baby sleeps. But I had envisaged napping with my child peacefully asleep in her basket by my side. Instead while I was supposed to rest or sleep, you carried your granddaughter almost all the time, tucking her into the *podaegi*[4] and rocking her to sleep while you cheerfully cooked and cleaned. In Korea this is quite normal; the grandmother or nearest female relative will generally come and live in to relieve all stress from the new mum. The baby is just brought to its mother for feeds. Rather than be grateful for your help, this enforced (because I couldn't explain in Korean that I didn't want it) separation from my baby roused a sort of lioness instinct in me. But I didn't want to offend you, so kept my anger and resistance to myself.

As a trained midwife, I knew the mechanics of lactation, but had little experience of how the emotional state of any individual mother can affect her breastfeeding. Keeping my feelings hidden, and subconsciously wishing my own mother were there instead, I became extremely tense. I felt that as a result of those feelings, my let-down reflex became slow and painful, and that my daughter suckled extra hard to make up for it. I experienced extreme sensitivity when nursing and in-between feeds for the following six weeks. My wonderful, more experienced midwife colleagues tried to help me see the problem but they couldn't remove the source of the stress for me. Others recommended stopping breastfeeding, but I felt this would mean appearing even weaker. I am so thankful that in spite of my at times silent, frosty manner as I processed all of this, you never stopped quietly supporting me. Although you couldn't encourage with words (our communication was limited to exclamations of 'big poo' or 'very wet' at nappy changing time, plus a lot of sign language), your actions in caring for me and my daughter revealed your manifest confidence that I would overcome these challenges.

Meanwhile, you seemed to be supergrandma! You awoke with the birds to make my husband's breakfast and packed lunch; you washed nappies and baby clothes by hand (to this day you are convinced it's the best way!). You even produced a whole range of Korean pickles for our store cupboard, all the while carrying the baby. I must admit I felt it was too much of an intrusion. I wanted to figure out my own way of mothering. For example: I wanted my daughter to learn to settle herself to sleep. At night I would put her down and pick her up repeatedly, infuriated that, as I thought, you had taught her to rely on being carried too much. Instinctively you knew all about what we in the West have labelled Attachment Parenting.[5] Your expectations and understanding of what a baby needs and is capable of were so different and (I now believe) superior to mine. As I persevered with sleep strategies from different parenting books, you hovered nearby with the endless offer of *ububa*?[6] Exhausted and simmering I would hand the baby back to you to settle her easily and deeply to sleep.

Of course, we did enjoy some lovely times too, when I forgot my secret grievances and peace reigned in the flat. I recall our shared pleasure watching *Murder She Wrote* together (you'd seen so many reruns in Korea that you knew the plots!). And shared laughter — do you remember in that third week we discovered I had somehow picked up head lice. Incredible! You had kept me isolated from the world for days so where had the little nasties come from?

Although communication was limited, over those long afternoons breastfeeding on the sofa while you hung up the washing and combed my hair checking for lice, I began to relax. Perhaps it was the endorphins being released? The peculiarly English sense of privacy regarding the body (and the scalp!) went by the wayside as I gave myself up to your care. You showed my husband how to massage me (thank you thank you!) and even how to hand express the milk when I was too weak with the alternating raised temperature and chills from mastitis. I had resented appearing feeble, but looking back I was unwell and emotionally very fragile. Thank you for seeing that and with your loving yet efficient approach getting me and my baby through that time.

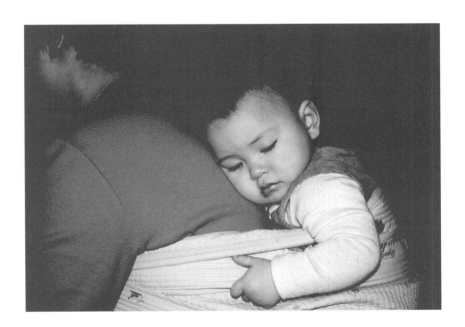

Photographs by Jinsoo Kim

These days I am enjoying the early weeks since my second daughter's birth. I have had no difficulties with breastfeeding and no head lice! You came over for a short visit and I was glad to let you hold the baby while I focussed on my pre-schooler. I've more or less embraced your style of mothering babies. I am a happy, confident *oma*[7] of two. (Still struggling with keeping on top of the housework though — how do you do it?!) Most of all, I think I've learned to apply some of the care and compassion you showed me, to myself.

From frailty to strength and joy.

With love and thanks

Louisa

LOUISA KIM

References:

1. *Omonim* translates literally as 'somebody else's mother' and is the Korean term of respect for any older woman who is a mother, including mothers-in-law, as in this case.

2. My idea was to write something that could be translated for my mother-in-law as a thank you gift.

3. For more stories of traditional Korean culture relating to childbearing, see: Fred Jeremy Seligson, *Queen Jin's Handbook of Pregnancy*, 2002.

4. Korean version of a baby carrier, wraps around the body like a short, thin duvet, compressing the breasts so ideal for grandmas, not so great for lactating mothers!

5. For more info. on Attachment Parenting see: www.askdrsears.com.

6. Can be translated as 'Shall I carry her on my back?'

7. Korean for 'mummy'.

Things My Mum Used to Say

Blow...
Come on if you're coming.
WHERE'S YOUR OTHER SHOE??
I love you more.
Wipe that muck off your face.
I couldn't get the bag you wanted so I got you this recycled one
from Oxfam instead.
Shut up, I'm watching Dallas.
By the light of the silvery moon...
I love you more.
You're worth 500 of him.
Charlie's dead.
You're so beautiful.
Is that a muffin top under there?
I wouldn't kick that Patrick Duffy out of bed.
I love you more.

EMMA COLEMAN

Mother's Hands

Mother's Hands
Her Hands;
Like gnarled, knotted
Olive trees...
Folded in her lap.

These are the hands
That held mine,
As I learned to walk.
These hands I hold...
Held me and soothed
A feverish brow
With tenderness.

They are the hands
Of one who worked;
Planting a garden
Canning the yield.

When did my hands
Become hers?
When did hers
Become her mother's?

ILAMAE STUCKI

Granny Coyne

My granny's a whispering woman,
her stories follow me down the hall;
hang, half-told, in the corners of the kitchen
above a tut-tut of metal knitting pins.

My granny's a soothing woman,
smoother of brows with a cool palm;
polisher of brasses; igniter of fires;
she picks up babies before they cry.

My granny's a loving woman,
shoes clucking on tiles when I call.
Her eyes laugh at me in photographs.
'She'd have loved you' my mother says.

ANGELA TOPPING

Remembering...

Maa.
Maatajee.
My name for you, it whispered to me that you were mine.
Like a kiss on the knee when I scraped it badly,
Better than any medicine the doctor could prescribe.
I was always falling over.
Maa! I would cry, and
You always came.

Mum, mummy.
These I called you in front of my school friends,
While my foreign tongue hibernated.
It made sense, having a secret name for you.
For me. Mum-me.

Remember that time
You made us jam sandwiches
When we played computer games?
You embarrassed me by telling us when our time was up.
And sometimes your black eyebrows went *up*,
Knitted into tight knots,
But never for long — I always said sorry.
You'd never tell dad.
(Mum's the word.)

Mama.
That's what I call myself now,
What my little girl calls me,
As I carry her around in an African-style sling.
Does she know that she belongs to me?

Mam.
This I might have called you once,
If we had all grown up in this country
If you hadn't come here from a faraway land,
To give me a better life.

You gave me yours.

But it doesn't really matter
What I called you then,
Or what she calls me now.
When all is said and done
There are no words to describe
Everything that you were, and still are to me.
That which is motherhood.

Mother. You are that, and so much more.

ZION LIGHTS

Cass and Jess
Drawing by Cassie Pearson (aged 14)

Our Children

•••

Letting Go

First you hold them like a secret
you only suspect is true.
Then soft knockings from within
tap out messages for you.
Slowly the body allows escape,
you hold them in your arms,
dazed and milky, full of love,
pledged to defend from harm.
Then you hold them to your heart
and put them to the breast.
But they learn to walk away
like any other guest.

ANGELA TOPPING

Being in Love

It's the smile,
the way it starts on one side,
not fully committed.
Bemused.
After eight short weeks
bemused?
The way the brave half
encourages the rest.
Wide grin sudden
and shocking in its absolute warmth,
full-mooned happiness.
No doubt.
Speaks from the soul.
Joyful wondrous new soul.

TARA O'DONOGHUE

Drops of Life

(for Aaliyah Obaahima)

Whilst these drops pour love and life,
your fingers twist your weaves
hold onto your cheeks, hold onto the breast for dear life.
Your hands soft under these winter-roughed lips. Breast milk,
neutral soap smell, sixty centimetres body long, delicate ears,
and nose and chin pierce through my heart, my soul –
God didn't send a child, He sent His most beloved angel.
Silent calling in the night, nudges the soul like a dolphin's cry,
strong infant body in my arms, like Mary in a manger,
the world vanishes as your lips get hold of the soft breast,
my star.
Tender kisses on warm curls, sleepy baby, my heart
take it, melt it like butter on fire, my life.

THEODORA A. A. IRESON

Mother, child, daffodils
Painting by Kathy Grossman

The Daffodils

The daffodils
Amongst the rills
Of water make
A scene to take
A nature lover's breath away.

And though the day
Will come when I
With adult eye
Will ponder, gaze
Upon that haze
Of yellow-green,
I'm still not keen
To shift my sights
To the delights
Of daffodils and springtime balm.

My mother's arm
Is all I need;
A milky feed,
Her shining face.
No other place
Provides such bliss;
She crowns me with a tender kiss.

MARIJA SMITS

A Day in the Life of a Six-Month-Old

Sometime in the middle of the night:
The room is dark and quiet, too quiet. Where is everyone? There's a funny feeling in my tummy that makes me squirm and fidget. I whimper, sucking my fingers, finding my thumb, but something's not right. I need my mummy. I'm all alone.

Just as I get ready to screech, warm hands grab me, lift me, and mummy's voice is in my ear, soothing, reassuring, and I relax. Mummy's familiar smell surrounds me and I latch on. We lie down together. Yummy warm milk fills my tummy and I drift back off to sleep. Every time I wake up, I nuzzle back in and mummy's milk is my reward.

7.00 a.m.
My eyes slowly drift open and I wriggle and stretch surrounded by the lingering, comforting smell of mummy. My hands seek soft flesh, but find only duvet and I frown. I can hear her voice in the distance. I smile at my big brother, who comes up to me and kisses me.

'Mummy, Markus is awake,' he shouts and grins at me.

'I've got him!' One of my big sisters swoops me up and happiness makes me giggle. I love my siblings. Next to mummy and daddy they are the best things ever. Gabs carries me off into the living room and I sit in my chair watching them all. They are doing that strange thing with a bowl and spoon again. Looks awfully complicated to me. Molly gives me a spoon and I happily munch on that.

Oh, there's the cat. Oh, hello mummy. Errr mum, mum, mum, where are you going? Mum? Ah that's better. She's picked me up and we spend some time just grinning at each other. I can't help but smile at mummy, and mummy always smiles back. Even better when she lifts her top and hmm hmmm, yummy, warm milk makes me sleepy.

8.30 a.m.
I jerk awake as mummy puts me down, and I protest. Who said she could put me down? Oh okay, she's putting the sling on. She laughs at me and I get all excited. I love going for walks with mummy in the sling. I'm right next to her, snuggled up under her coat and I can see everything. The cold air hits my face and I turn into mummy's neck.

She smells so good and I kick my legs and shove my hands under her arm pits. Now that is cozy. I watch the funny white stuff float by and giggle at Molly playing peekaboo with me. Mummy slips a few times, but it's okay. I know I'm safe in here, all cozy and warm and…

9.15 a.m.

I open one eye and mummy smiles at me as she's putting me down. I don't want to be put down, but I'm too sleepy to say, so I drift back off. I wake up in my chair in front of the telly. I can hear mummy talking to me as she is doing that strange thing she calls housework. She doesn't do a lot of it, which is my fault apparently. Well, I just want my cuddles, what do I care what the house looks like?

9.45 a.m.

She is taking far too long with this housework thingy and I'm getting restless.

'I'm coming,' she says. 'No need to get your nappies in a twist.'

Easy for her to say. I'm hungry now and talking of nappies… Just as I get really agitated mummy is there.

'Hey, it's okay, silly sausage, I'm right here. I'm all yours now.' I grumble and snuggle into her. We play peekaboo whilst she changes my nappy. I wonder what toxic waste means?

That done mummy sits down and I nurse, falling asleep again to the sound of her tapping away at the computer. Mummy does that a lot. She's a writer you see. Don't ask me what she writes, not for little ears apparently, but I don't mind. I get nice long snuggles with her when she does that, 'cause she forgets to put me down.

11.15 a.m.

Mummy's alarm goes off for the nursery run and we grin at each other. I've been awake a while now, bopping on and off the boob and trying to help mummy write. I think I pressed something I shouldn't have 'cause mummy screeched and put me down for a minute. Now I'm waving to grandma on Skype. Mummy is on there almost as much as something called Facebook and she giggles a lot. So I giggle too, 'cause I like it when mummy is happy. She puts me in the sling and we're off to get my big brother. I'm all excited, because Tj is such fun to watch and play with.

12.15 p.m.

I'm back on the boob, but keep getting distracted. I want what mummy is having. I give up on the boobies and swipe mummy's sandwich off her. I keep dropping it and get frustrated, so I hold mummy's hand to make sure she holds it up to my mouth. Hmmm tastes nice, but I spit most of it back out again, getting us both covered. The banana isn't much better, nice to suck on though.

Mummy laughs at me as I get crosser and crosser and settle for mummy's milk instead. Ah that's better. Mummy's milk is the best!

1.30 p.m.

Playing with mummy and Tj is such fun. Peekaboo is still my favourite though. Makes me dissolve into giggles every time. All that playing makes a boy hungry. I need more mmm mmms. Mum, mum, mum? Where has she gone? Ooh the dog... What was that? Can I eat it? Mum? Mum? Mummy picks me up just before my face hits the floor. This sitting up lark sure takes some getting used to. Hmm, did I say I love my mummy? I bob on and off the boobies and giggle. I bite down and mummy tells me off — whoops — sorry mummy. But my gums hurt and it feels so good to chew. Oh no she's putting me down, no, no, sorry mummy. Phew, she's picked me up again, I best nurse properly, hmm, yum, I can never keep my eyes open and I'm so sleepy...

3.00 p.m.

We're off again on another school run. I woke up when mummy put me down to put the sling on and I needed a quick top up, so now we're running a bit late and mummy is walking really fast. This is fun and I get all excited when I see Gabs. I flirt with mummy's friends and make them laugh. Though why everyone else has to stare at mummy as though she has three heads I do not know. Well, technically she has two heads of course, mine and hers, but really. I wouldn't want to be down there in one of those buggy things. Much prefer it up here, it's so cozy.

4.00 p.m.

I went back on the boob the minute we got in. Everyone else is eating biscuits, which I'm not allowed to have, so I am going to stay here in protest. Every time mummy tries to put me down, I am making my

Doodle by Angie Stevens

feelings clear. She distracts me for a bit by putting me into the door bouncer. Hey this is fun, bounce, bounce, bounce. But all that bouncing makes me hungry. Mum! No you can't cook dinner in peace. I need you, now… hmm mummy's milk, yum, yum, yawn…

4.40 p.m.
What? She put me down? Mum! Ah that's better, boobies, yum. No, don't put me down, no. Hmm yum, more boobies — no really mummy, please don't put me down. I'm tired and hungry and tired and actually I have no clue. I just want a cuddle. Oh goodie, she's putting me in the sling. Now I can watch her whilst she cooks dinner. Oh the cat, oh Tj, hmm thumb. I might just have a little snooze whilst I'm here. No, I need more boobies.

5.30 p.m.
Daddy! Did I say daddy is my next favourite person after mummy? Mummy says he always manages to walk in when she serves up dinner. Daddy says I'm his big boy sitting in the highchair all by myself. Now what is this squishy stuff he puts in front of me? Oh look, I can chase it around the tray. Hmm, apparently it's called spaghetti bolognese and why is everyone laughing and saying I've changed colour? Splat, splat, oh what fun.

6.00 p.m.
All that chasing food made me hungry so I'm back on the boobies. Minus my clothes, 'cause they got all sticky and now it's bathtime. I do like splashing in the bath. Gabs holds me and we spend ages in there. Mummy keeps complaining that we make the floor all wet and I just giggle. Just as I get fed up mummy is there with my towel and she dries me off and gives me a massage. Hmm, bliss. Not sure who likes this more, mummy or me, and it makes me so sleepy.

7.00 p.m.
Am getting all fidgety and cranky, 'cause I'm tired and everyone keeps grabbing me when I only want mummy. Finally, she sits down and I attach myself. I have every intention of staying here for some time, so mummy best not think about trying to put me down.

8.00 p.m.

Help, where is she? Oh, hello daddy. We grin at each other for a bit, but I keep rubbing my eyes and I really want my mummy. Why does she have to sort out clothes? Doesn't she know I need her? Some wild animal may come and snatch me when I sleep and I'm hungry again. Starving in fact, so... Oh hello mummy. Did I say I really love mummy's milk?

10.00 p.m.

What am I doing in here? Where is... oohh yummy, mmm milk.

11.30 p.m.

I'm just about to protest, when I smell mummy and hmmm yum.

Sometime in the middle of the night:

The room is dark and quiet, too quiet. Where is everyone?

And so it continues...

DORIS O'CONNOR

149

Numnee

'Numnee' is Sophie's all-purpose word for breasts/milk/nursing

Numnee is lovely
Numnee is sweet
Numnee is lovely
Numnee is neat.

SOPHIE WOOD (aged 4)

Drawings (clockwise from top left) are by: Kira Cornell (aged 9), Cassie Pearson (aged 11), Salomé Wendling (aged 7), Rebecca Bellamy (aged 4), Cassie Pearson (aged 13), Salomé Wendling (aged 7).

Slow Down Mummy

Slow down mummy, there's no need to rush,
slow down mummy, what's all the fuss?
Slow down mummy, make yourself a cup of tea.
Slow down mummy, come spend some time with me.

Slow down mummy, let's pull boots on for a walk,
let's kick at piles of leaves, and smile and laugh and talk.
Slow down mummy, you look ever so tired,
come sit and snuggle under the duvet, and rest with me awhile.

Slow down mummy, those dirty dishes can wait,
slow down mummy, let's have some fun — bake a cake!
Slow down mummy, I know you work a lot,
but sometimes mummy, it's nice when you just stop.

Sit with us a minute,
and listen to our day,
spend a cherished moment,
because our childhood will not stay!

REBEKAH KNIGHT

Mum
Picture by Rebecca Bellamy (aged 4)

Nolwen, Nine Months Old

I know we should not make
sentimental statements about babies

after all, you are a person, not a thing;
you have your dignity, though small.
You make your fair share of mess and noise,
you keep older people awake at night;
you suffer pain, all windy stomach
and teeth cutting through raw gums;
you roar at carved stone lions,
tweak the cat's ears, and you have, I am told,
already eaten sixty-four different foods

but to a faraway grandma
you are pure apple blossom,
pink and white, petal soft,
with twinkly cornflower-blue eyes,
rowanberry hair and breath
as delicious as wild thyme. In fact
you are a perfect bunch of sweet-pea joy.

JULIA PRESCOTT

Skin

Light shines through
the package in ultra-thin covering
snuggling on my knee.

Firm, plump, soft, embracing
the perfume of a fig that's ripe for eating:
I bury my nose to inhale your sweetness.

Leaning against my breast
and dreaming down the years,
your small, strong fingers fondle mine,

discovering and pulling at
the folds of loose flesh on my hands
that surprise me, unite me

with generations of incredulous women
who learned from the wisdom of their grandchildren
that they were on their way to growing old.

ALWYN MARRIAGE

Poem for Sylvie, aged eleven months

She has slain me with her waking,
Pulled me gasping from my needy deeps
Into a grey light filled with birdsong
And babbling.

How could I leave her crying on the shore
While I slip back into sleep's inviting waters?
She, my beaming baby,
She, so heart-breakingly pleased to see me.

She has not let me sleep well for a year.
These words are hard-won from an arid brain,
But something about the complicity of 5.40 a.m.
Demands to be documented.

She is a babbling brook,
Pure well-head, spontaneous font
And I am scratching on all fours
In the dry earth.

So when inspiration bludgeons me,
Cudgels my brains out from behind,
It hits me with a line meant for another day.
Concusses me.

A line that rings in my head like tinnitis,
Distracting, unwanted, un-relating,
Pulled from a different depth
Like my metaphor.

I dig on,
Wringing familiar words for drops of freshness.
For her, it's a whole new day.
Never the same river twice.

ALICE ALLAN

Blackberries

Let me lift you
high in my arms,
your cheeks stained
with blackberries and tears,
your hands stung by nettles.
We'll sit
in the dust
amongst the stones and weeds
and I will lift you
through your tears
onto my lap.
Little hands
fumble, furious,
through layers of clothing.
I help you
and hold you to me,
your body tight,
mouth trembling,
searching for my breast.
At last, found,
limbs loosen,
sobs subside,
eyelids gently curve into sleep.
You lie
plump and heavy
across my knees
grubby and so so soft.
Your lips fall away from me
and you smile
in the secret solitude
of blissful
blackberry-full sleep.
Such a welcome, blessed burden
my child, my love.

ALISON PARKES

It All Fits Together

It is 11.30 p.m. on the eve of your first birthday, and I am here, in my pyjamas, sitting on the floor in front of the hearth. I am surrounded by a bewildering array of lengths of wood, a variety of screws and fixings, and a few rather confusing pieces of paper. I am going to build you a rocking horse.

It's late and I am tired, much like the night you were born. Now, as then, I find a surge of energy buoys me up, a great wave of passion; however tricky this may be, I can't give up! The thing is though, the instructions are somewhat lacking; it's not really clear what fits where and if I do it wrong, the whole thing won't work.

I pause and gaze at you in miniature on the screen of your monitor and feel the familiar sensation of power rising in my breast; I am missing you, even though you are fast asleep and dreaming upstairs. I look back at the instructions again and slowly, gently, begin to breathe, to be, to allow things to come together.

This is like the first time I was with you, alone, about two hours after your birth. We'd gazed at each other, then slept soundly, side by side; that shocked blackout sleep of relief and elation, of recovery and preparation. I woke as you did, but I didn't know what to do; in my hazy sense of surfacing, of coming to, I realized that I didn't know what the instructions were. A friendly face, compassionate hands helped me to place you closer, skin to skin, as we had been only so recently; but what now? I looked down and was almost blinded by the love in your eyes, overcome by the feelings welling up inside me, wishing all good things for you, all joy, all blessings.

You didn't seem to know that we might need instructions, or, if there was a manual, you certainly hadn't needed to refer to it. You, a being so tiny, you just knew. We lay together, a small constellation, linked not only by the light of our love, but by the flowing energy of life force between us; the amazing colostrum emerging to give you gifts of immunity and protection. There in those small hours of darkness, as you spent your first night outside attached and nursing, I realized that we didn't need a manual.

We are lucky in our dance of nursing. In rhythm so far, we have followed each other's steps; you leading, me following, our footprints, large and small inside one another. We nearly come to our anniversary little one.

I look down at your sleeping face and my busy hands, assembling, trying screws in wood, tightening, testing the strain, adjusting, repositioning. Now I know what manuals and instructions are for, yet when I struggle with any part of the process, it's your father I call for; a gentle second opinion, an affirmation shared, or a correction softly offered.

Each time we place the pieces together, check back, confirm accuracy, it becomes easier. We can see things finally taking shape, and when we accidentally fasten one rocker on upside down, we remove it and begin again. There is no shame, we are learning together. Happy, we climb to where you are; remembering those first nursings, the depths of your eyes, our tears of joy, and anticipate your smiles at this, your birthday gift. It all fits together.

ALISON JONES

That's My Son

That's my son.
He's just turned one.
I can't believe how far he's come.

Everything I know,
I'll show him.
Every journey I make,
I'll take him.
Every seed I sow,
I'll grow him.
Every recipe I read,
I'll feed him.

Every song I hear,
I'll sing it.
Everything he needs,
I'll bring it.
Every story I know,
I'll tell it.
Every word I write,
I'll spell it.

And still, with all this to learn
he gives me more in return.

Every noise he makes,
sounds like a song.
Every time he sleeps,
he rights a wrong.
Every tear he cries,
time stands still.
Every time he trusts,
he spreads good will.

When he claps his hands,
I'm thunderstruck.

When he laughs,
I'm lifted up.
When he moves,
it looks like art.
When he smiles,
he steals my heart.

That's my son,
he is the one
who makes me feel,
life's just begun.

JUDITH HURRELL

Smiler
Photograph by Teika Bellamy

Quietly Enthralled

I am
quietly enthralled,
as
swan wing lashes rest
over golden hazel glow
and wonder shapes a curving smile...

a sigh — lost adrift a comforting embrace,
a restless hand held safe in mine...

in this reverberating nighttime reverie
of one he so resembles,
my child sleeps,

a Universe of love
within my arms.

TERRI STUTELY

Painting by Cassie Pearson (aged 13)

A GCSE in Parenting?

Before I became a mother at the relatively advanced age of thirty-two few of my friends had had children of their own; my mum once joked that I wouldn't know one end of a baby from another. Both my grandmothers were the oldest of six children and were no doubt experienced in caring for their younger siblings. As for me, I'd held a couple of babies before my son was born, but knew very little about them. Surely, I wondered, there should be some GCSE in parenting that all prospective parents should have to pass before being allowed to procreate? In the absence of such a qualification, my husband and I attended antenatal courses, where we practised putting a nappy on a doll and learned how to bathe and dress a baby. I bought a book that modestly billed itself as a babycare bible.

Attachment parenting; babywearing; co-sleeping, were all terms that were only vaguely on my radar before I became a mother. I never imagined that our son would cry if we placed him in his Moses basket at night, only to fall asleep in my arms, or that he would reject his cot in favour of our bed. I had a vague idea that at six months he would easily make the transition to his own room, where he would sleep soundly for twelve hours. I thought that I'd have him weaned shortly after his first birthday. But he had other ideas.

At eleven months, he got his first proper cold. Breastmilk kept him going when he ate little in the way of solid food. Sometime after his first birthday, he lost interest in feeding during the day and I thought we were well on the way to weaning. After another cold, however, he decided he quite liked having daytime milk after all. I've yet to find a better way of calming him down and comforting him when he cries after bumping his head.

'Before you know it, he'll be doing his GCSEs,' our neighbours said to me once. I try and keep this in mind when he's woken up for his fourth night feed, trying to relish the closeness co-sleeping and breastfeeding bring before he gets to an age when I'm no longer the centre of his universe.

As I write, he has just started to take tentative first steps. At the moment, he's walking towards me, ready to fall into my arms, but it won't be long before he's running away to play, knowing that I'm there waiting for him. As he grows up, I'll try and always hold on to the memories of him squealing with delight when I put him on my back, smiling at me when I carry him on my front or holding out his arms for a cuddle. And I'll remember his eyes gradually closing as he drifts off to sleep during a feed, nourished and comforted by his mother's milk.

SARAH BURGESS

Drink your milk, little girl

A lullaby

'Drink your milk, little girl,
like the buffalo calf,
drink your milk, little girl,
like the buffalo calf in the field...
Like the pup from the wolf
like the cub from the bear
like the foal from the mare
drink your milk, little girl, Whisper Rose...'

SOPHIA BASAN

From Sophia's story 'Wakan Yeja — The Sacred Being'

Illustration by Cassie Pearson (aged 15)
Inspired by a photo in Baby Milk Action's 2011 calendar

Exactly

My rising star.
My Bear-Child —
Oh, enchanting little one!
I do not want this time to end,
I must preserve you, precious friend,
Exactly as you are.

My special girl.
My new-found love —
You know not what you did:
A silent stowaway one night,
Enshrined in love you clung on tight
Exactly where you were.

My Soul mate.
My enchantress —
So infused with awe at life;
Your precious eyes so wonder-filled
Whence sparks and such bewitchment spill,
Exactly from your heart.

LUCY HOLMES

30th March 2011
For Caroline Kallisto, with ALL my love xxx
(Kallisto became the Great Bear constellation in Greek
mythology)

A Letter for When You Are Grown

My Darling Daughter,

As I write this you are dozing peacefully on your daddy's tummy, my little toddler worn out after a hard day's adventure. I know in a while you will slowly wake, rubbing your eyes as they adjust to the soft light and moistening your dry lips with a few small flicks of your tongue. You'll come over and nestle in my lap, snuggling up close for your 'boo'. After a few quick sucks you'll get going and relax back into your rhythmic feed. It's the most natural routine yet it amazes me every time.

I love feeding you, I really do. I always knew that I wanted us to breastfeed. I looked forward to it with nervous excitement, not quite sure how we'd master our new skill but confident we'd get there somehow. I trusted you to know what to do, just the same as you trusted me. Together we would find our way.

In your first precious moments out in the world you lay on my chest, warm skin so soft and sweet, snuffling about for your first proper drink. It was incredible to see you find your way onto my nipple and give it a little test with your tiny mouth! I felt so proud of you for knowing exactly what to do, and proud of my body for providing you with what you need. In those few moments I knew we would be okay. We were bonded together; relationship cemented through this mutual nourishment for body and soul.

Now as the months swiftly pass we are still going strong. I never imagined we would get this far and I wouldn't change it for the world. Our breastfeeding journey is the most magical and intimate experience of my life. I'm so proud to be sharing this with you and so grateful to you for giving me this chance. Nothing has ever made me feel so special and right. It's empowering yet humbling; the most important and worthwhile thing I have ever done yet so enjoyable and effortless at the same time. Nursing you fulfils me at such a deep level that I eagerly drink in every second of this blissful experience while you do the same taking your fill at my breast. It's like time stops and for those few minutes it's just you and me in the world. Our little pauses, day and night, where we drop out of reality and into our special warm cocoon of perfection. Connected in all senses of the word whilst we both recharge our spirits.

I know one day you'll start to move on and our breastfeeding journey will gently end. You are an amazing girl and already have so many great qualities shining through which I know will only get brighter as you grow. You are happy and loving, adventurous and feisty, caring and warm. You love playing with baby dolls and stomping about with dinosaurs. You smile at everyone but sometimes act shy which only goes to make you even cuter. You are happy to run off and play, to climb about and explore, and I watch with pride at the independent child you are becoming. I know you will come back to me when you need me, clambering up on my lap asking for 'boo, pleesh'. Or just pulling on my shirt and trying to get in there yourself because I'm not being quick enough and you're really thirsty, right now! You know I am here to give you that safe, warm, secure feeling of emotional comfort as well as a full tummy and from that I know I've done right by you.

As these months turn into years I want you to know how much our early relationship means to me. I want to make sure that when you are grown you can read this and know just what an amazing life we have always had together. It's been liberating for us to be able to go wherever we want and when you've needed a feed we'd just do it. We've fed in the car, on a plane, in different countries, on the beach, in the snow, in the library, at a rock concert. And that's just so far! I can't wait to see what comes next.

Breastfeeding has been such a formative part of our relationship and given me so many memories that I will cherish forever. I will remind you of them all I'm sure and when you get fed up of hearing the same anecdote for the umpteenth time I hope you'll still feel the love it passes on. You may no longer be nestled in my lap but my arms will always be open and waiting. A safe, warm, secure base for you to come back to whenever you need.

I love you my Sweetpea, heart and soul. I always will.

Mummy xxx

DAWN CLARKE

To My Daughter

You gave ground to my longing,
balance to my hope.
You smoothed out all the spaces
that made me doubt
and wish for something different.
You gave me belief
in myself
and of a higher power.
You gave me the strength,
the courage,
and the will to carry on.

I waited for you for so long
lessons broke through the sidelines
and I learned that gifts are granted
when they are also received.

IDA KOLLER

Unbreakable

Hard to believe now
that we are such separate beings —
you a great strapping
toddler of three, all-knowing,
I a hopeful extemporizing
mother.
Thankfully, when you were born
and we parted for the first time,
we kept that close touch.
Feeding fed us both
with love and care
and slowly, only when ready,
you drew away to other
sources of nourishment.
But the everyday miracle
is still there in my memory
of the closeness between us
and of us and in us
and the sweetest, most gentle
bonds are unbreakable.

CATHY BRYANT

Fledgling
or
A first experience of birds

Birds had always been: somewhere,
above, beyond —
small restless things which chirped
and disappeared.

Now they were
cloud spread just below;
he so close to
sheeny, bustling buds
of folded wings!

Magic-ring eyes aglance
they shally,
ruffling, twisting.
In spirals,
small fingers curl...
breath over-brims...

Then a step.
A gallopette.
A skip — and a flurry!
And out across the park a charge
of driven, beating glory!

And as the birds he follows
take flight above
beyond his reach —
he raises hands
and beats them
down and up;
feathers like lashes gleam,
winging into the sun.

*

Those pigeons have long flown.
Yet now, with thoughts that fire:
they pour within!
still fluttering...
and, driven as a bird,
his forearms beat,
eyes glow, breath fills,
until, on tip-toe poised —
new winged words fly.

RUTH ASCH

May Dawn, Devon

My daughter's fingers draw and pull
A tangle of birdsong into thread,
Weaving the dawn chorus
Into the fabric of her memories.

In the damp light
The singing is as green as moss.
Moss-felt, padding the ache of separation,
Muffling and softening sharp edges.

My daughter is calling back to the birds
As the valley mist rises.
Three generations of our family are waking to her birdsong.
This is home.

ALICE ALLAN

Home

My wearied feet print all the world
In endless journey through,
So far from home, the ones I loved,
And all the things I knew.

Wherever I wander in this world,
Wherever my feet shall roam,
In unheld hearts and unseen lands
I'll find what is my own.

In strangers' arms my mother's touch,
My friends when all alone
In strangers' eyes my father's face,
In all my pathways, home.

JAMES PICKLES

Flowers
Art quilt by Karen Bachman-Kells

The Ballad of the Beach

I walked along a golden beach,
Awash with stones and shells.
I felt the sand beneath my feet
And heard the children's yells.

I watched my daughter run ahead
To climb a grassy dune;
I gladly followed where she led,
For well I knew too soon,

She'd be too old, 'grown up' she'd say
To share these things with me,
And then I'd be here all alone,
Just staring at the sea.

So wanting very much to keep
This moment evergreen,
I took in all the sights and sounds
The seen and the unseen.

This memory-to-be got saved,
And fixed within my brain,
The way we laughed and "misbehaved";
The sudden fall of rain.

Now years have passed, my daughter's grown
And gone beyond my reach,
But when I close my eyes and *pause*
We're back there on that beach.

MARIJA SMITS

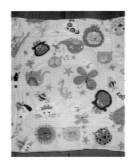

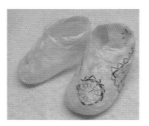

Clockwise from top left: Knitted hat and fingerless gloves by Rebecca Edmonds, Baby booties by Tara O'Donoghue, *Grub, A Way of Love* mini quilt (front and back) by Liz Edwards ('grub' is their family term for breastfeeding), Dolly Doula and Knitted boobies by Kirsten Millinson, Baby booties by Tara O'Donoghue, Bag by Libby Jonson, Cup cakes and LLL cake by Gillian Mabbitt. Centre: LLL embroidery by Miira Dawson.

Afterword

by Anna Burbidge,
Chair of La Leche League GB 2007 — 2012

A mother is something that we all have in common, but she is also unique to each of us. One of the things that I appreciate about La Leche League is the acknowledgement that each mother and child's relationship is unique. As a young mother I found I received a great deal of advice about what I should or should not do. Much of it did not feel right to me but I felt I should listen to those who seemed to know what would be best for me and my baby.

I found out about La Leche League in a series of lucky moves, randomly ordering *The Womanly Art of Breastfeeding* from a magazine and then moving to an area where one of the first LLL groups was running and recognizing the name on a poster. In another turn of fate I phoned the number on the poster the day before a meeting and the next evening, eight months pregnant with my second child, I found myself at my first LLL meeting.

It was to be an evening that changed my life. All of a sudden I was hearing mothering being talked about in a way that felt right to me, not in a way that gave advice or laid down rules, but that spoke about listening to myself and my baby and doing what felt right for us. I had no idea that evening that thirty-seven years later, and with six grown up children, LLL would still be a key part of my life.

First and foremost, because of the information and support I got from LLL I was able to happily breastfeed my babies. More than that, LLL gave me the tools to grow as a mother, and to have the ability to learn from each new baby with their unique personalities. I learnt not to assume that what worked for one baby would be right for the next, and I loved watching my relationship with each child grow. I didn't always get it right but I knew that if I seemed to have got it wrong I could admit it and look for a different way to respond. LLL's belief that we look at what each child is able to cope with at any particular time guided me through school days and teenage years, and prepared me for my children becoming adults and going out into the world and making their own choices.

LLL Leaders are all on their own unique path of motherhood, but we share a common bond of mothering through breastfeeding and whenever we meet it is like finding an old friend. Coming along to a La Leche League meeting opens a door to a whole range of musings on mothering and no matter how long a woman is part of LLL or how much she wishes to take from our philosophy, she will always be welcome. From those mothers who need no more from us than a chat on the telephone to those who go on to become Leaders and make LLL a part of their lives, LLL is there to offer suggestions and support to fit in with our unique relationships with our children.

Wooden carving by an unknown sculptor
Photograph by Teika Bellamy
With many thanks to Lisa De Souza who owns the carving.

Acknowledgements

I am indebited to all the contributors who gave so generously of their artistic and literary work. I thank each and every one of you for adding your own unique creations to this book. Your voices are strong!

I would also like to thank all the mothers, LLL Leaders and other creative folk who gave me support and encouragement. And to all the "invisible" people on forums who helped me over the hurdles I encountered with desktop publishing and website creation. Especial thanks go to Ruth Lewis and Emma Gardner for taking over the production of *Feedback* in my absence.

I am also grateful to my own wonderful mother, Ludmila, who has supported me in every venture I have ever undertaken in my life. Also, I give my thanks to my mother-in-law, Pat, for her help and enthusiasm.

And finally... I would like to thank my husband, Tom, for putting his trust in me and this project. Also, for making me cups of tea late at night.

***

I would like to acknowledge the following kind people for permitting me to include their previously published work:

Kathy Grossman: 'Green Peppers' was originally published in LLL of Western Pennsylvania's *PennsyLLL Points West*, Spring 2000. 'To the Stars and the Moon' was originally published in LLL of New Mexico's *Enchantment*. Kathy's illustrations and paintings have regularly appeared in LLL publications, and along with her poems, are reprinted by permission of their creator.

Petra Hoehfurtner: An earlier version of 'Tears in Her Eyes' was published as 'Breastfeeding — A Woman's Right' in LLLGB's *Feedback*, Spring 2009. 'Tears in Her Eyes' is reprinted by permission of the authoress.

Pauline Kirk: An earlier version of 'A Modern Madonna' was published in *Perceptions: an anthology of poems by women celebrating women's lives*, edited by Peggy Poole, and published by Poetry Monthly Press, 2000, and also in *Hear Our Voice*, edited by Natalie Nightingale and published by Women's Words, 2001. Reprinted by permission of the authoress.

Sheila Kitzinger: 'The Crowning' is from *A Celebration of Birth*, published by Pennypress, 1986. 'The Crowning' and Sheila's batik *Birth* are reprinted by permission of their creator, Sheila Kitzinger.

Alwyn Marriage: 'Skin' was first published in *South* poetry magazine in 2006, and also in Alwyn's collection *Touching Earth*, published by Oversteps Books in 2007. 'Skin' is reprinted by permission of the authoress.

Guy Meynell: Guy's painting was first published in *Painting With Words*, published by The Provost and Fellows of Eton College, 1990. The painting is reproduced by permission of the Provost and Fellows of Eton College.

Alison Parkes: 'Love Potion' was first published in *LLLGB News* March/April 1999 and 'Homecoming' was first published in *LLLGB News* March/April 1997. 'Blackberries' and 'Happy Birthday!' were first published in *LLLGB News* September/October 1996. These poems are reproduced by permission of the authoress.

Cassie Pearson: Cassie's illustrations have appeared on a regular basis in *Breastfeeding Matters*, and all of her artwork is reproduced by permission of the artist.

James Pickles: 'Home' first appeared in the chapbook, *To My Friends*, published in 1995. This poem is reproduced by permission of the author.

Lisa Scott: The photographs 'Christabel & Zachary', 'Emma & Josiah' and 'Tracy, Shaun & Teyla' taken by Lisa Scott (www.lisascottphotography.com) are from *The Rugby Breastfeeding Café* 2010 Calendar. Many thanks go to Rosie Evans, who has ownership of the images, for permitting me to use them. The breastfeeding calendar was a fundraising initiative which Rosie organized so that peer support training could be purchased for interested mums at the breastfeeding café. You are one amazing lady, Rosie!

Terri Stutely: An earlier version of 'Quietly Enthralled' was published in *Such Words As These*, edited by Ben Johnson, published by Ravenshead Press, 2012. The poem is reproduced by permission of the authoress.

Angela Topping: 'Ultrasound' and 'Last Gifts' first appeared in Angela's collection *Dandelions for Mothers' Day*, published by Stride, 1988. These two poems as well as 'Granny Coyne' appeared in Angela's collection *The Fiddle* published by Stride, 1999. These poems as well as 'Letting Go' have been reprinted by permission of the authoress.

Allthough every effort has been taken to trace and communicate with all copyright holders before publication it has not always been possible to do so. In case of any errors or omissions please contact Teika Bellamy at the earliest opportunity.

Hat designed by Lisa from www.lactivist.co.uk.
Photograph by Kelly Gerrard

Alice Allan

Ruth Asch

Shireen Babul

Lucy Benton

Benaifer Bhandari

Cathy Bryant

Caroline Cole

Clare Cooper

Helen Cooper

Cindi Eastman

Betsy Finn

Kirsten Foubister

Index

of Artists and Writers
with Select Biographies

Alice Allan (30, 154, 172)
I am a writer, lactation consultant and La Leche League Leader living in Addis Ababa, Ethiopia. I have two children, aged 5 and 3. My eldest daughter was born in Japan, far from my family, so I know how vital the support of other mothers is, and how rewarding it is reading about their experiences.

Nazmin Akthar (10)
Lawyer by day with a keen interest in matters of equality and diversity, a writer by night, and everything else I wish to be or do in between.

Ruth Asch (170)
Ruth Asch is a some-time teacher (of English and Latin), wife, mother and poet. She has taken extended parental leave in order to breastfeed and now homeschool three children (David, 7, Miriam, 4, and Joseph, 1). She published a first volume of poetry in 2009, entitled *Reflections*, with St Austin Press, and in rare moments when inspiration and time enough coincide, is working on further poetry and poetic translations for future publication.

Rachel Ashe (106)

Shireen Babul (51)
Shireen is a passionate primary school teacher, aspiring writer, blogger, baker, enthusiastic school librarian and most of all a wife and mother. She is a soulful city dweller and lives in London, U.K., where she finds inspiration of all kinds. Her happiest days are spent picnicking in the park with her husband and daughter, Mira.

Karen Bachman-Kells (Front cover, 26, 174)
Karen Bachman-Kells, RN is an artist who lives in Chicago, Illinois. The inspiration for her art quilts has come from serving families through her profession as a home birth nurse. Karen's passion for these women and their babies is lovingly stitched and pieced into each work in her mama art quilt series. To see more of her work, go to: Karenscraftyworld.blogspot.com.

Sophia Basan (164)
Sophia was born and raised in East Germany. She has lived in the U.S. for 22 years and has been writing all her life.

Rebecca Bellamy (150, 151)

Teika Bellamy (159, 178)

Lucy Benton (108, 109)
Lucy Benton has a Creative Writing degree from The University of Chichester. She writes at: theprincesspoetslifeadventures.blogspot.com. She lives on the Sussex coast with her husband and son. She is a breastfeeding peer supporter.

Benaifer Bhandari (27, 67)
Benaifer Bhandari lives in Hertfordshire and is passionate about home education, homeopathy and mothering through breastfeeding. She is a published poet who adores writing about the things that interest her and in particular, the divine qualities of mother nature. She can be contacted through benaiferbhandari@gmail.com.

Lynn Blair (48)
Lynn Blair is married to David and has four daughters. She writes in a little yellow hut in the corner of the garden, has published in *Juno* magazine and is a part-time lecturer in the Academy of Creative Arts in Reid Kerr College. She can be contacted at lynnblair@hotmail.co.uk.

Cathy Bryant (47, 169)
Cathy Bryant's poems and stories have been published on five continents in magazines and anthologies. In 2010 she won the Marple Humorous Poetry Prize and in 2012 she won the Sampad 'Inspired by Tagore' Poetry Contest and the Swanezine Poetry Competition, and became runner-up Prole Laureate. Cathy co-edits the annual anthology *Best of Manchester Poets*, and her own collection, *Contains Strong Language and Scenes of a Sexual Nature* is available from all good booksellers or online. She can be contacted at cathy@cathybryant.co.uk.

Charlotte Buchanan (62)
La Leche League were a huge help to Charlotte Buchanan as she found her way with breastfeeding her eldest. Wanting to share the joy of breastfeeding and make things better for struggling new mums, Charlotte trained and volunteered as a peer supporter. She now has three children and lives in Woking in Surrey.

Sarah Burgess (162)

Alejandra Cerdeño Lance (19)
I was born in Mexico City, studied in Mexico and in Plymouth College of Art and Design, U.K. I have a Ph.D. in Multimedia; I specialized in photography underwater as well. I came back home after that and worked, and still live in Mexico. Photographer since 1990 my web page is: www.alejandracerdeno.com.

Dawn Clarke (166)
I'm a full-time mother and live in Cambridgeshire with my husband, daughter and stepson. I like reading, writing, rock music and biscuits. I always wanted to be a Mummy and now that I've got the chance I really am living the dream.

Caroline Cole (20)
I am a 31 year old full-time Mum to Ewan James, who was born in June 2010. I am a lactivist, and an active member of La Leche League Derbyshire. As a freelance journalist I write passionately about natural parenting issues for magazines and my blog, on topics including breastfeeding, babywearing, bedsharing, travelling with children and natural living: www.stoneageparenting.com.

Emma Coleman (v, 133)
Emma lives in Bromley, Kent with her husband and three crazy sons. She has written short stories and poems since she was a child, and likes to write about every day subjects, twisting them into something absorbing and surprising.

Clare Cooper (119)
I am the mother of two beautiful daughters who fill my life with laughter and joy, and who are the inspiration for my writing. I am a pregnancy yoga teacher where I use yoga to empower and inspire women during pregnancy and help them to connect with their baby and prepare for birth. I am the co-founder of Beautiful Beginnings, a natural parent and child group which celebrates and supports breastfeeding and natural, responsive parenting in West Cumbria.

Helen Cooper (96)
Helen is the mother of two wonderful girls, as well as being a freelance editor and writer. She is an advocate of natural/attachment parenting, and writes about the challenges of remaining mindful whilst juggling motherhood and self-employment at: www.zenmummy.co.uk.

Tomas Cynric (68)

Jim Dawson (70, 121)

Josie Devine (50)
Josie Devine is a primary school teacher living in Co. Kildare, Ireland. She writes poetry and short stories. She wrote the poem 'Earth Mother' for her daughter on the birth of her first child.

Cindi Eastman (80)
Cindi Eastman is a mother of two beautiful healthy boys, Leland, 3 and a half, and Jesse, 13 months. She breastfed Leland for 25 blessed months, and will continue to nurse Jesse for as long as she can. Along with her husband Chris, the family reside in Winnipeg, Manitoba, Canada. Cindi's other passions in life are cooking healthfully for family and friends, reading a good book and spending time outside with the wee ones.

Betsy Finn (79)
Betsy Finn is a mother, wife, and artist who lives in Michigan. Her photographs and portraits have won international acclaim, and along with her writing, have been published in blogs, magazines, and books. Her website is: bphotoart.com

Kirsten Foubister (73)
Kirsten Foubister is a stay-at-home mum to Ruaraidh (4) and Orla (1), living in East Lothian, Scotland.

Alexandra Florschutz, MA (8, 13, 75, 102, 118)
Alex paints about being a Woman – a journey to find the Source of a woman's power, the feminine spirit, which thrived in the more female-oriented cultures, only to be superseded by the patriarchal way of life. She wonders how women can retain the true nature of their gender while navigating our masculine driven world. Alex has been on an exciting journey of self-discovery and shares her passionate insights into themes such as conception, birth, feminine sexuality and how this can also be represented in the cycles of nature and life. Visit www.florschutz.com to see more of her work.

Emma Gates (65, 127)
Following her graduation from Kent Institute of Art and Design, in 2002 with BA (Hons) Photography, Gates went on to teach Photography and Art & Design at different academic levels, alongside creating and exhibiting new work in both solo and group exhibitions. Gates started on an MA Photography at the end of 2009 and completed the flexible mode in 2011 after the loss of her mother and birth of her first son in the same academic year.

Gates' work is based nearly exclusively on autobiographical subjects and all of her work is made through a compulsion to record and create an archive. Recording things from the mundane to the monumental to create a memory, in case (and when) we start to forget.

Kathy Grossman (xii, 45, 58, 117, 142)
Kathy Grossman was accredited as an LLL Leader in 1985 and lives, writes, and paints in Moab, Utah, U.S.A.

Teodora Graham (37)
Teodora graduated from the National Academy of Fine Arts N. Pavlovich in Sofia, Bulgaria. She works as a freelance paper conservator, artist, and full-time mum near Cambridge, U.K.

Nik Harris (39)
Nik lives in Motspur Park, near Kingston and Wimbledon with her husband Jethro, Olivia aged 6 and Bea aged 3 years. She helps run two monthly LLL meetings locally.

Lisa Hassan Scott (34, 85)
Lisa Hassan Scott is a full-time mother of three children aged 9, 6 and 2. In her spare time she is a writer, Yoga teacher and La Leche League Leader. She blogs about mothering and the mind at: www.lisahassanscott.co.uk.

Laetia Hawksby (60)
Laetia Hawksby lives in Stoke Newington and is a stay-at-home mother to a lovely little daughter. She makes no apologies for being unreservedly sentimental and romantic.

Barbara Higham (40)
La Leche League Leader Barbara Higham lives in Ilkley, Yorkshire with Simon and their three children Felix, Edgar and Amelia. She is Managing Editor of *Breastfeeding Today* for La Leche League International and co-edits *Breastfeeding Matters* for LLLGB.

Petra Hoehfurtner (103)
I am a La Leche League Leader and my contribution came out of observations and conversations I had with women over the years in a variety of settings. I added to that some Gestalt Therapy Philosophy and this is what I ended up with. If you would like to leave a comment, please feel free to go to my website: petrah.co.uk/Articles — and post it there or you can send me a private message over the contact page.

Lucy Holmes (66, 165)
In addition to being a budding children's author, I am a 38-year-old full-time Mum to our 2-year-old little girl, a sustained breastfeeder (still going strong at 25 months), LLL member and *The Mother* subscriber, an ex-Police Officer; I helped run a hotel in Mexico, worked for the NSPCC, did corporate hospitality in London and have also managed the park and grounds at a stately home in the U.K. (amongst other things)! My husband is an RAF officer and we have an almost deaf and blind 16-year-old dog. We sadly have not yet discovered our own Paffley the Dem (per my picture stories) to go adventuring with at the weekends!

Lisa Hassan Scott

Barbara Higham

Lucy Holmes

Theodora A. A. Ireson

Marzana Islam

Sarah James

Judith Hurrell (158)

Theodora A. A. Ireson (33, 43, 141)
Theodora is a writer and lifestyle blogger. After five years living in London, U.K., she is currently living in a small city in Canada with her husband, and their newborn daughter. She loves to travel, photographing and writing her experiences in her journals.

Marzana Islam (15)
My name is Marzana Islam and I am 20 years old. I am a BA(Hons) Illustration student currently in my second year studying at London Metropolitan University.

Sarah James (82)
Sarah James is a poet and mother of two energetic boys. Her first poetry collection *Into the Yell* (Circaidy Gregory Press) won third prize in the International Rubery Book Award 2011. She is currently working on her second collection. Her website is at: www.sarah-james.co.uk.

Ben Johnson (83)
Ben Johnson lives in the New Forest, Hampshire between the forest and the sea though he doesn't view either as often as he would like. He enjoys quiet pursuits such as reading, walking, gardening and running an online poetry forum. When he gets time away from those he attempts to write poetry.

Alison Jones (17, 18, 156)
Alison Jones is a mother, poet, teacher, storyteller and musician. Her interest in writing springs from listening to her mother reading aloud as a child and to this day. Alison works as a teacher, inspiring her pupils with the dance of words, the magic of film and the power of stories.

Alysha Jones (42)
Alysha Jones is lucky enough to have worked as an LLL Leader in the United States, in the Azores Islands, and in England, and to have been able to travel many places with her wonderfully supportive husband and two little girls, Emmalee, aged four, and Hanna, 21 months old. She graduated from California Polytechnic University in 2004 with a Bachelor of Arts in English with an emphasis in Poetry. She and her family, including two very well-travelled Border Collies, are currently living in Norfolk, England, and love it there.

Lisa Katz (100, 101)
I am a mother of two children, now five and two years old, a British citizen who emigrated to New Zealand, trained and worked as a counsellor, and am now a full-time mother, fitting in creative writing as much as I can.

Louisa Kim (128)
Louisa Kim is a Community Midwife, currently taking a break to be with her two girls.

Jinsoo Kim (131)

Pauline Kirk (75, 84)
Pauline Kirk lives in York, and is the author of three novels: *Waters of Time* (Century Hutchinson), *The Keepers* (Virago/Little Brown) and *Foul Play* (Stairwell Books), the last written as PJ Quinn. Ten collections of her poetry have been published, including *Walking to Snailbeach: New and Selected Poems* (Redbeck Press). Her poems, stories and articles have appeared in many anthologies, and been broadcast on local radio. She is also editor of Fighting Cock Press, and as a performance poet has appeared at venues and festivals throughout the North. A second PJ Quinn novel, *Poison Pen*, is due out later this year.

Sheila Kitzinger (22, 23)
Sheila is a social anthropologist of birth, birth educator and writer.

Rebekah Knight (151)
Rebekah Knight is a creative, Christian mum from London. Rebekah enjoys being creative, and also travelling, socializing, art, writing and trying to be all that she was created to be! Rebekah is the mother of three daughters, Jessie-Jane, Ellie-Faith and Giorgia-Evie. She is married to James. Together they are enjoying finding the purpose and joys of everyday life. If you enjoyed this poem please visit Rebekah's blog at: http://rebekahknight.blogspot.co.uk. The devotional blog offers advice, family stories, reviews, poems and a journal of thoughts on everyday life as a Wife and Mother.

Ida Koller (168)
Ida Koller lives with her two young daughters and husband in a small mid-coast Maine town. In college she decided all she wanted to do in life was to write and have babies, and thus far she's loving it all. Ida can be found at http//:onceuponatime-ida.blogspot.com or http//:stellas-star.blogspot.com.

Rita Kornell (110)

Judith Kuegler (55)
Though born in Germany to German parents, Judith Kuegler grew up among tribal communities in Nepal and Indonesia. Her interest in creating art began at a very early age and is profoundly influenced by her multicultural upbringing. After attending Art College in Germany she moved to the U.S. to continue her studies in art and psychology. Judith works as an artist and writer specializing in global women's issues, multiculturalism and anthropology. She lives with her two sons in North Carolina.

Her work has been featured in a variety of publications such as, *Victoria* magazine, *American Scientist*, *Motherverse*, *Juno*, *Journal of the Association for Research on Mothering* and *New Beginnings*. Judith participates in the annual 'Changing Faces of Midwifery: Birth Art Show' at the East End Gallery as well the Carrboro and Hillandale Art Walks, MOMart and Whimsical Women. She blogs about art, motherhood and everything in-between for *Motherverse* magazine and *Mama Says Zine*.

Zion Lights (136)
Zion Lights is a writer and mother interested in feminism, ethics, and green living. She has a one-year-old girl and they still enjoy breastfeeding, co-sleeping, babywearing and attachment parenting. She lives in the West Midlands with her small family and an assortment of rescued animals that she couldn't resist taking home.

Zion is a regular contributor at *The Huffington Post* and *One Green Planet*. Other published articles can be found via her website: www.zionlights.co.uk and she can be followed on twitter@ziontree.

Pippa Little (12)
Pippa Little was born in East Africa, raised in Scotland and now lives in Northumberland, North East England. She has three collections, *The Spar Box* (Vane Women), *Foray: Border Reiver Women* (Biscuit Press) and *The Snow Globe* (Red Squirrel Press). *Overwintering* comes out in October 2012 from Oxford Poets/Carcanet press.

Alison Lock (74)
Alison's poetry has won prizes, commendations or honourable mentions in: the Virginia Warbey Competition, the Nottingham Open Poetry Competition and in the collection and single poem categories of *The New Writer* 2010 Prose and Poetry Prize. Her poems have been published in several magazines and anthologies including *Reach Poetry, Dawntreader, Indigo Dreams Crab Lines Summer Anthology, Visible Breaths* and the *Soul Feathers Macmillan Anthology*. She was Poet-in-Residence for the Holmfirth Arts Festival 2012.

Riona Mackin (32)
My name is Riona Mackin and I'm the mother of two sons, James (5 years old) and Jude (11 weeks). I'm 33 years old and work as a French teacher. I live in Northern Ireland and am married to Gary. I have breastfed both sons (still going strong with Jude!) and it has been the most satisfying thing I've ever done. I adore it and have encouraged close friends to do it.

Alwyn Marriage (153)
Alwyn Marriage's seven published books include poetry and non-fiction. She has read at many festivals and events in Britain and abroad, and her poetry appears frequently in magazines and anthologies. Alwyn has been a university lecturer, editor of a journal, Chief Executive of two international NGOs and an environmental consultant. She is now Managing Editor of Oversteps Books and research fellow at Surrey University. www.marriages.me.uk.

Emer Martin (90)

Claire Mills (46)
I am 40 years old, happily married to Greg and we have two gorgeous children; Ella and Ben. I am an Infant Massage Instructor and breastfeeding peer supporter.

Maryam Mirza (31)
I am Maryam, mother of baby Arthur. I learnt to draw in Leicester, which is where I grew up. Drawing has enabled me to capture precious moments of my son. I would like to continue drawing and developing my work and ideas!

Guy Meynell (123)

Alice Meynell (116)

Arthur Molloy (59)
Born in the Republic of Ireland, Arthur was lucky to meet and marry the love of his life Siobhan back in 2006. They currently live the good life (most of the time!) in the Isle of Man with their two boys and a third expected in December.

Anna Morton (24, 29, 95)
My name is Anna Morton and I became a mother in 2009 with the birth of my daughter Freya Mary Kiekie. I loved being pregnant and had a beautiful home birth which was the most incredible experience of my life, it was for me a spiritual awakening. Since then I have been writing poetry and prose as often as I can and have been generally keeping to the theme of the spiritual journey of motherhood, from pregnancy onwards. I breastfed Freya until she was 15 months old and I became pregnant with her brother, Escher. I have often found that ideas for writing come most freely during the sacred time of feeding my children — the space for mothers musing!

Bob Mundell (124)

Allen Ng (43, 56)
ANG Photography provides a range of event and portraits services to clients in Avon, Gloucestershire, Midlands, Wiltshire, Somerset, Devon, Dorset, Berkshire, Oxfordshire, Hampshire and South Wales areas. Services include charity/fancy dress balls, proms, corporate events, mother and baby portraits, family portraits and relationship portraits. www.ang-photography.com.

Doris O'Connor (144)
Doris O'Connor is a mum of nine, and has been breastfeeding continuously for the last nine years. Breastfeeding is just what happens in her house every day. In her other life Doris writes steamy, erotic stories on her trusty netbook. You can find Doris on the web here: www.dorisoconnor.com.

Tara O'Donoghue (140, 176)
I'm a mother to three strong, beautiful, happy boys aged from 7 months to 13 years. I loved birthing at home, nursing my babies and watching them grow. I live in West Cork, teach baby sign language; sometimes I get time to create.

Rachel O'Leary (76)
Rachel is a co-Leader of LLL Cambridge. She is also an International Board Certified Lactation Consultant, grandmother, and storyteller.

Alison Parkes (78, 89, 92, 155)

I've been an LLL Leader since 1988. Having a family with my husband Robert has been a real joy, and my poems were written for my children, Gareth, Duncan and Lorna, who are now grown up.

Lucy Pearce (52)

Lucy Pearce is mama to three young children and lives on the East Cork coast in Ireland. She works as a free-spirited freelance writer and is a regular contributor to *Modern Mum* magazine, *The Irish Examiner* and *Juno* magazine, where her column, Dreaming Aloud, has run since 2009. Online she contributes to *Rhythm of the Home*, *The Anti-Room* and *Wild Sister* magazine. She is contributing editor at *Juno*.

Her first book *Moon Time: a guide to celebrating your menstrual cycle* is available from Amazon.

She blogs at www.dreamingaloud.net on living philosophy, moon time, everyday zen and gentle parenting. Her website www.thehappywomb.com features Woman-craft: honouring moon time, women's circles, creativity, rites of passage, natural pregnancy, holistic birth preparation and so much more.

Asha Pearse (vi)

Asha creates beautiful images of motherhood and the family bond; celebrating and promoting natural parenting through her paintings. She also works as a designer and illustrator. She lives in Oxfordshire with her husband, son and their cats. To see more of her work visit: www.worldsofwhimsy.co.uk.

Cassie Pearson (138, 150, 161, 164)

Cassie Pearson is a young artist. She illustrated the LLLGB members' magazine Toddler/Mum to Mum columns from the age of nine onwards. She can be contacted on: cassiemarie_p@yahoo.com.

James Pickles (173)

Julia Prescott (25, 152)

Julia was born and brought up in Cambridge. She lived in the U.S.A. for 2 years and has now been in Scotland for 35 years. She studied Archaeology, taught English to A-Level grade and now paints, gardens and writes. She has two daughters and six grandchildren.

Nadia Raafat (86)

Nadia is a mother of three. She breastfed and co-slept with her two sons, now aged 9 and 7, until they were 2 years old. She is still co-sleeping with and breastfeeding her daughter, aged 3. Nadia is the co-founder of BatterseaYoga, SW London where she teaches pregnancy yoga, birth education and mum and baby yoga. She is also a fully registered and practising Birth Doula and runs The Magnetic Mothers Circle — a monthly social and support circle for attachment mums. She loves the poetry of Louis MacNeice and Carol Ann Duffy, Middle Eastern Cooking and a good cup of chai tea in bed.

John Roe (14)

Nayla Ruiz-Salfity (i)

Scoop (126)
Scoop is a full-time mummy and wife living in Rochester, Kent, U.K. She is also a broadcast journalist called Suze Cooper. She has been writing in rhyme for as long as she can remember and self-published her first book of poetry in 2011. It is called *Mumology* and is full of poems inspired by the first year of her son's life.

Lisa Scott: www.lisascottphotography.com (71, 74, 77)

Alex Simon (81)
The Softest Place on Earth is a photograph of my wife breastfeeding our 13-month-old son. It won an amateur photography competition in which nudity of any kind was prohibited, but the subject matter was deemed appropriate, and men and women alike found it beautiful.

Marija Smits (28, 88, 143, 175)
Marija is a poetess, writer and mother-of-two. Her writing has appeared in various publications and when she's not busy with her children she's busy writing. You can find more of her work at: www.marijasmits.wordpress.com.

Katrina Soper (57)
I am an LLL Leader living in South Wales with a husband, four children and too many pets. I love cooking for hungry friends and am also trying to learn the violin — I have the honour of being my teacher's oldest student. One of my ambitions is to find the time to write more than three lines!

Michelle Sorrell (9)
Michelle Sorrell lives in East Anglia with her husband and son. She enjoys walking along the coastline, days out with the family, good food, reading and writing poetry. She reads everything and anything, loves to paint and wishes her garden would look after itself.

Jessica Starr (44, 114)
Jessica Starr healer, writer, doula, crafter, teacher, artist, trainee breastfeeding counsellor, wife of Neil, Mother of Ella. For more about Jessica please visit: www.patchworkmama.co.uk.

Michelle Steele (ii)

Angie Stevens (4, 72, 147, back cover)
Angie Stevens is an illustrator most well known for her sketchbook blog, Doodlemum. She qualified from the University of Westminster in 1996 with a degree in Illustration. Angie lives in Swansea with her husband Myles and her three children Millie (9), Evie (4 and a half) and Gruff (2 and a half). She is very proud to have breastfed them all well into their second year. Angie is also a trained breastfeeding peer supporter and is very passionate about women's feeding choices in regards to their children.

IlaMae Stucki (134)

IlaMae was born and raised in the Salt Lake Valley in Utah, in the U.S. She is a registered nurse of 25 years and now helps children in special education at school. Her hobbies are reading and writing poetry, jewellery making and sewing. She has been married for 42 years to Ken who teaches science.

Terri Stutely (160)

Terri has one son and has always enjoyed expression through prose and poetry. She likes to read (science-fiction and fantasy) and enjoys living by the sea immensely. She spends most of her time with her son.

Angela Topping (16, 122, 135, 139)

Angela Topping is a freelance poet who lives in Cheshire. She has six poetry collections and three chapbooks to her name. Many of her poems are based on her experience as a daughter and as a mother. Her most recent collection, *Paper Patterns*, is forthcoming from Lapwing. She also writes for children and her most recent children's book is *The New Generation* (Salt 2010).

Jo Welch (38, 43, 94)

Jo Welch (Wood) was born in Nottingham in 1970. She was also educated in Nottingham City where she focussed her studies in the arts and music. During her adolescence, Jo swam competitively for England and Great Britain and was world ranked in her event. As Jo moved away from swimming during her early 20's, she refined and developed her artistic talents, designing knitwear and studying for a degree in fashion design. In 1995, Jo opened a shop called 'Spirit' in Nottingham's Flying Horse Walk Mall where for over 5 years she sold thousands of individually designed hand painted glass pieces.

In 2000, she moved on from the high street shop into a studio gallery in Nottingham's Lace Market until 2002. She then followed her interest in Gestalt Psychotherapy and studied with Birmingham University. Jo loves photography, creates digital art and is passionate about expressive dance, engaging with the dancing path known as 'The Wave' originated by Gabrielle Roth. Jo also creates sequenced music with flute and vocals. Her passion for visual art is currently focussed on making mixed media painting reconstructed as abstract collages, painting on glass and photography. She exhibits her work in Sherwood, Nottingham at 'A Room Full of Butterflies'.

In 2010, she gave birth to her son James Gabriel. Jo strongly supports breastfeeding relationships including the feeding and nurturing of an older infant or toddler. She trusts that by following her son's interest in continuing to feed, that this is fundamentally what he needs to do for optimum health and development. Jo believes that breastfeeding provides emotional and physical nourishment and that it is a divine gift of love.

Jean-Mathieu Wendling (120)

Sophie Wood (150)

Alysha Jones   Lisa Katz   Zion Lights

Pippa Little   Riona Mackin   Claire Mills

Anna Morton   Doris O'Connor   Lucy Pearce

Julia Prescott   Scoop   Angela Topping

About La Leche League

La Leche League is an international non-profit, non-sectarian organization which, for over 55 years, has been dedicated to providing education, information and mother-to-mother support and encouragement to women who want to breastfeed.

La Leche League Great Britain (LLLGB) has been offering mother-to-mother support in Great Britain for 40 years and has 80 groups and 250 Leaders. LLL Leaders are mothers who have themselves breastfed for 12 months or longer and undergone an accreditation process. They know that breastfeeding is not always easy and how much difference having someone to talk to can make. Leaders provide telephone counselling, email support and local group meetings, as well as leaflets on a wide range of breastfeeding questions, information on more unusual situations, access to a panel of professional advisers, and they can often lend out books covering various aspects of pregnancy and childcare.

For further information about LLLGB please visit the website: **www.laleche.org.uk** which includes an online helpform that enables a mother to receive email help from an LLL Leader. Or, if you want to talk with a Leader, you can phone our **helpline number**, **0845 120 2918**. All our Leaders are volunteers and answer calls from home while looking after their families.

***

ALL ROYALTIES FROM THE SALE OF THIS BOOK WILL BE
DONATED TO LA LECHE LEAGUE GREAT BRITAIN